Lessons from a Chief MARKETING OFFICER

WHAT IT TAKES TO WIN IN CONSUMER MARKETING

Bradford C. Kirk

McGraw·Hill

New York   Chicago   San Francisco   Lisbon   London   Madrid   Mexico City
Milan   New Delhi   San Juan   Seoul   Singapore   Sydney   Toronto

658.8
K59L

Library of Congress Cataloging-in-Publication Data

Kirk, Bradford C.
  Lessons from a chief marketing officer : what it takes to win in consumer marketing
  / Bradford C. Kirk.
        p.   cm.
    Includes index.
    ISBN 0-07-140317-5
    1. Marketing.   2. Advertising.   3. Marketing—Management.
  4. Advertising—Management.   5. Marketing research.   I. Title.

  HF5415 .K5243   2003
  658.8—dc21   2002035359

Cau

1 2 3 4 5 6 7 8 9 0   LBM/LBM   2 1 0 9 8 7 6 5 4 3

ISBN 0-07-140317-5

McGraw-Hill books are available at special quantity discounts to use as premiums and sales promotions, or for use in corporate training programs. For more information, please write to the Director of Special Sales, Professional Publishing, McGraw-Hill, Two Penn Plaza, New York, NY 10121-2298. Or contact your local bookstore.

This book is printed on acid-free paper.

For Lisa, Jackson, and Tyler

Contents

Contents

Contents

Preface

Lessons from a Chief Marketing Officer is written for current and aspiring consumer marketers, including brand managers, marketing directors, and VPs of marketing. It's also valuable reading for those who work with consumer marketers—people in advertising, publicity, marketing research, R&D, sales, packaging, finance, operations, and top management.

Although many of the lessons presented here apply to all marketers—business-to-business and services as well as consumer products—most of the examples are drawn from the most marketing-driven of all industries: packaged goods. This is the domain of such marketing powerhouses as Procter & Gamble, Kraft, Unilever, Nestlé, and PepsiCo. Their insights and experiences allow you to learn from the best.

Lessons from a Chief Marketing Officer is written by a real-life chief marketing officer. I'm not a consultant or agency guy and never have been. For twenty-two years, including eight as a chief marketing officer, I've been responsible for delivering share growth and capital-efficient profits. The lessons in this book are about what actually works on the front lines of marketing, not what could or should work. I hope you find these lessons useful.

Acknowledgments

Thanks to Barry Richardson, formerly of Hope College, for fanning the original flame of marketing passion in me, and to Phil Miller of Howard Miller Clock Company for giving me my first chance to put it into practice. Thanks to Brian Sternthal, Bobby Calder, Sid Levy, and Dick Clewett for all your help at Northwestern Business School.

Thanks to Andy Bresler, Barb Schneider, Chip Matthews, Stu Haugen, Dave Buck, Dave Stevenson, Jessie Barach, John Sweetwood, Tom Touhil, and Blair Gensemer of Ralston Purina for your great examples of innovative marketing and for your mentoring. Thanks to Rick Frank, Lynda Robleski, Bob Thomas, Gene Zeffren, Pat Hambrick, Andrea Saia, Jon Achenbaum, Stan Cook, Karen Moberly, Maureen Collins, Ralph Blessing, Gail Lanznar, Gil Smith, Chuck Cooper, Ron Gidwitz, and all the other great marketers/leaders at Helene Curtis—we had quite a run, didn't we? Thanks to Gabi Weiler and her team at Henkel. Thanks to Bob Dellelis, Jon Richmond, Pat Wyatt, Steve Feldstein, and Bill Mechanic of Twentieth Century

Fox for giving me an "establishing shot" in entertainment marketing. Thanks to Carol and Howard Bernick and the rest of the management team at Alberto-Culver for helping me *really* think like an owner, as well as to Cecil Hinkhouse, Stu Morse, Tom Monaghan, Janice Miller, Pam Harting, Laurie Schulte, Mike Puican, Soni Simpson, and their teams for putting this into action. Thanks to Bill Gentner and the entire management and marketing team at Andrew Jergens. Good stuff is happening!

Thanks to all the great advertising agency people who always kept job number one clearly in focus: Carl Spielvogel, Debra Pawlick, Eric Weber, Terry Gallo, Charlie and Marlene, Katalin Kavogo, John Kaiser, Chris Zimmerman, Bob Scarpeli, Judith Wormey, Pam Mikulec, Frank Ginsburg, Tom James, Ernie Brown, Donna Wiedekehr, Rick Gibson, Shelagh Brooke, Glen Jacobs, Tom Bernardin, Gary Epstein, Nadine Peterson, and Paula Foreman (who always asked, "What if it works?").

Thanks to the pals who have always helped to put it in perspective: Bené, Chazmo, Bobo, Tylermon, Lord Rothrock, Spitto, Otto, Johnnie(s), Romage, and Sal.

Thanks to my agent, Ethan Ellenberg, and my editors, Danielle Egan-Miller and Anne Knudsen.

Thanks to my wife, Lisa, and sons, Jackson and Tyler, for their constant encouragement and support.

And special thanks to my parents, Cy and Roz Kirk, for their love and for modeling purpose and persistence in everything.

Lesson 1

Personal Characteristics of Successful Marketers

Succeeding in marketing requires an unusually broad skill set. One morning, you are making a new-product presentation to two hundred salespeople, brokers, and senior managers. Later that day, you are listening hard as a group of women discuss their reactions to your latest TV ad. Later still, you need to make a quick decision on whether to ship or scrap a run of product that is slightly off its quality specifications. The daily reports that overflow your in-box demand that you fully grasp statistics and accounting essentials. Reviewing new package designs, you must be a master of aesthetics. The list goes on and on.

Over the years, I have been fortunate to work with dozens of great marketers. On many levels, they have been as different from each other as people can be. Yet they all shared three characteristics that set them apart from their peers. To begin with, they were all natural leaders. It wasn't just that they had the habit of command, although they did have that. They inspired and motivated, leading others to achieve more than they imagined possible. Every great marketer I have met was also eternally curious, resulting in an ability to foster innovation in every marketing task. Finally, their appetite and, yes, passion for consumer insights, for market-dislocating programs, for results was exemplary. I believe that leadership, innovation, and passion—wrapped up in the acronym LIP—are what it takes to win at consumer marketing.

Leadership

Marketing leaders set good direction for their brands, communicate this direction tirelessly, and treat every investment in accomplishing this direction as if the money were coming out of their own pockets, just as a sole proprietor would. Along the way, as part of their leadership, they manage the day-to-day workflow with excellence.

Setting and Communicating Direction

Your first job as marketing leader, as brand CEO, is to establish a destination for your brand—that is, a brand destiny. Think of yourself and your team waking up in the middle of the desert with one fundamental question to decide: which way to start walking. You can't stay put, and you can pick only one way to go. You sniff the wind, scan the horizon, poll the team, feel the sand, check the sun, inventory your resources, study your compass, send out scouts, and then make the call. Translated into marketing terms, you study your financial statements, understand your brand's role in the corporate portfolio, survey your consumers, scout out the competition, scan adjacent markets and channels, evaluate the current and prospective performance of your product and creative, and make the call.

Good marketers give good direction. That direction incorporates big aspirations, but it must be firmly rooted in reality. A powerful brand vision needs to be based on a clear-eyed assessment of the brand's and company's current position, strengths, and weaknesses relative to the competition. It needs to incorporate an internally consistent and plausible set of assumptions about the future, including such considerations as category growth rates, consumer trends, technology development, and new competitive entrants. It needs to delineate an appropriate time horizon. Think of John F. Kennedy's 1963 call for putting a man on the moon and returning him safely to Earth by the end of that decade.

Richard Ferris, former CEO of United Airlines, provided famously bad direction for his company and his brand. He tried to go against the most basic reality—that United is an airline—and turn it into a travel company instead. Before he was fired, Ferris had combined the airline with rental car and hotel companies and changed the name to Allegis. BIC, the maker of low-cost pens, disposable lighters, and disposable razors, somehow entered a reality distortion zone that led the company to believe it could sell low-cost fragrances as well. L'eggs used an innovative direct-to-store delivery system to build a strong panty hose business. The company mistakenly thought the same method would work for cosmetics (L'erin). Procter & Gamble speculated that its marketers could evolve Olay from a skin-care brand to a total beauty-care brand and consequently lost hundreds of millions of dollars on Olay Cosmetics—after five years of test marketing, no less.

On the other hand, P&G determined that Tide was a total detergent brand, not just a powdered detergent. The launch of Liquid Tide mortally wounded Wisk, the one-time king of liquid detergents. Likewise, over the years, Gillette has created a new reality for itself, moving from a razor brand to a "male grooming" brand. Colgate has been redefined from a toothpaste brand to an oral-care brand, incorporating toothbrushes and mouthwashes.

While most of these examples seem obvious in hindsight, none of them were foregone conclusions at the outset. The consequences of being right or wrong are very high indeed. Identifying the most *realistic* and *appropriate* direction for your brand is the essential first step.

Once you have fashioned a strong direction for your brand and sold it to top management, you must hardwire it into your brain and the brains of everyone on your team. Every new opportunity, every new piece of research, every new investment needs to be filtered through the lens of your brand's direction. That direction becomes the key decision criterion, the gatekeeper. Consumer product organizations are simply too large and too complex to effectively take the whiplash of constant change. There are only so many

Errors of Omission

It's easy to spot big mistakes that show up in the market-place. These are the errors of commission. But many of the biggest failures of vision never make it to market. These are the errors of omission—the things that should have happened but didn't. Why isn't Palmolive in the skin-care business in the United States? The brand is strong in this category in many other countries but not in the world's richest consumer market. Why was P&G thirty years behind its rivals in going global? And why isn't Pep-siCo, with its direct-to-store delivery prowess, in the cookie business in a big way?

person-hours and investment dollars available. You need to make choices. You need to, in effect, blinker yourself from so much of the commercial noise we all live with. Find your direction, then focus, focus, focus.

Having a compelling brand direction does much more than help you sort out what not to do. It also helps generate on-strategy options to exploit. When your suppliers know what you want, they get much better at providing it. When your team knows what will be acted on, they get much better at providing actionable recommendations. Good direction lights a fire; it animates, it inspires.

Unfortunately, hardwiring others with your vision is incredibly hard to do. We all communicate far less than we think we do. To have a chance of infecting others with your brand's directional vision, to have other people see the brand through your eyes takes repetition, and it takes simplification. You need to create a brand "stump speech" that you use and reuse every opportunity you get. You need to stay consistently, predictably on message. You need to make your message as short and memorable as a mantra.

Ideally your message is so pithy and expressive it can be boiled down to a single hand gesture. Winston Churchill's victory *V* is the classic example. I once used three fingers raised on each hand to communicate a number-nine brand's share goal of being number three by 2003. Whenever I saw the CEO in the hall, we used this gesture to greet each other. For a brand we were overtly milking, I got the sales force to make a "barnacle" gesture with their hands (all fingers bent as in a grip) plus a Jack Nicholson–in–*The Shining* growl to communicate the importance of holding on to valuable shelf space until replacement products were ready. The point is to somehow, anyhow, get out the word and feeling on your brand direction.

Acting Like a Proprietor

I have had the pleasure (and occasional peril) of working for three multibillion-dollar, family-controlled (though publicly traded) companies. In all three, the founder or founding family was still very much in charge: the Gidwitz family at Helene Curtis, Rupert Murdoch at News Corporation (owner of Twentieth Century Fox), and the Lavin/Bernick clan at Alberto-Culver. In each case, employees at all levels could feel the visceral willpower of those at the top. These leader/owners all had chips on their shoulders, a raw determination to succeed, and an utterly Faustian expectation that they could have their way with the world. They didn't do what they liked to do or what they were good at. They did what needed to be done. Of course they acted with a sense of proprietorship—they owned the joint. And of course they acted with a long-term view—they were all thinking of their kids and of their legacies.

All the successful marketers I've known have this same unbending willpower and proprietary sense. Regardless of their place in the hierarchy or the size and priority of their particular businesses, they are incapable of letting inertia, pride, or comfort keep them from their appointed rounds of pushing, pulling, and cajoling the business ahead. They have an internal gyroscope that gives them the confidence to do what's right, by their lights, regardless of the obstacles. And they are so persistent and consistent in their drive that no one ever accuses them of bullying or of spouting things they think the boss would want them to say. The brand is their master, and they just enforce everyone's submission to it. Proprietors don't think about effort, they concentrate on results. Their mind-set about spending money is that if the investment doesn't work, they and their children won't have dinner that night.

Managing with Excellence

The final dimension of marketing leadership is nothing more (and nothing less!) than managerial excellence. Planning, organizing, and controlling. Completed staff work. Rigorous establishment and updating of performance objectives. Recruitment, training, and retention. Management of meetings (agendas, the right participants, recaps). Team assignments. All the elementary managerial hygiene required to get the railroads to run on time. Today's hyper-lean staffing and the relentless need for speed make mastering these basics harder than ever. So does globalization. So does the increased scrutiny from Wall Street. So do consolidations and acquisitions.

The most important sources of managerial and, therefore, leadership advantage come from the near-zero-based assessment of how to get the right things done well. Look at your calendar and those of your management team. Are you scheduling enough time to think, to innovate? Do you really need the weekly, monthly, and quarterly staff or business results meetings? Or can you modify the participant list significantly? Why do the sales and marketing people work on different floors? Have you bitten the bullet to let your star person get that development rotational assignment? Are the development process and document format for the annual marketing plan as productive as they need to be?

Pulling off managerial excellence in today's environment requires rethinking what is needed from past practices—that is, deciding what can be jettisoned and what must be added. This requires as much innovation as product development does.

Certainly there are some new tools that can help. Almost every office employee now has a personal computer at his or her desk. Technology's productivity potential is still huge relative to what's been realized at most organizations—with marketing organizations often on the trailing edge. If you're not using your computer network to schedule meetings, store always-accessible key documents (such as marketing research reports), access real-time media plans, graphically portray sales and share data, and manage the new-product development process, you are being left behind by your competitors. The same holds if you're not using videoconferencing, digital asset management systems, and consensus forecasting tools. These are all just "table stakes" tools, the dial tones of managerial excellence in the twenty-first century.

Innovation

If there is a Zeus in the pantheon of words that consumer marketers must bow down to, it is certainly *innovation*. Even in the most hidebound, reactionary companies, innovation is the proclaimed, if not always honored, deity. In truly progressive companies, innovation is the animating spirit driving everything, especially differentiation.

By now it is, of course, accepted that innovation can come from anywhere, inside or outside the organization. Don't let R&D have a monopoly on this word. Today, innovation on your brand can't just be accepted from all functions, it must be demanded. A healthy brand requires a robust stream of well-channeled innovations of all sizes targeted against your chosen direction.

"Grabbable" Innovation

Often, innovation opportunities are just sitting there, waiting to be picked up and used. I call this *grabbable innovation*. One of the most fertile areas for grabbing innovations is advertising claims. Often you can simply preempt or even "postempt" (bring back something from someone's archives) claims that are the proverbial low-hanging fruit. John Smale paved his way to the chairmanship of P&G by getting the American Dental Association's endorsement of Crest and then advertising this fact constantly.

Suave is now the Wal-Mart of health and beauty care. For the past generation, it has been a textbook case on how to market a successful value brand (there is a data-rich Harvard MBA case study on it). The innovation that ignited Suave's growth was comparative advertising back in the mid-1970s. Suave's "Ours does what theirs does for less" head-to-head comparative advertising required no exotic research, no expensive test marketing. It just took a hungry marketing team willing to disregard the inertia, customs, and habits of the industry at that time. The Federal Trade Commission's (FTC's) ban on comparative advertising had been lifted for quite some time, so this type of opportunity was open to everyone. Suave just took the lead, preempting everyone else.

Advertising for Old Spice antiperspirant postempted the time-tested but recently neglected tactic of offering a money-back guarantee, with great results. Years before, Dove did the same thing with the age-old "seven-day test." Many brands have grown their share simply by advertising that they won a readers' poll in such magazines as *Allure* or *Good Housekeeping*.

Media plans are another good arena for grabbable innovation. There was no law that said TV commercials all had to be sixty seconds long when Leonard Lavin insisted on buying thirty-second spots. Similarly, there was no law against it when he insisted the networks sell him free-standing fifteen-second spots twenty years later. His motto was and is, "Winners make it happen." The resulting media plans worked better for Lavin's scale of business.

When he was head of the home video unit at Disney, Bill Mechanic and his team created an innovative distribution strategy called "disappearing hits." They systematically released, removed, then rereleased classic Disney animated videos such as *Snow White*, *Pinocchio*, and *Cinderella* on about a seven-year cycle. This created scarcity—and massive demand—without shooting another frame of film.

Packaging also is a fertile source of grabbable innovation. Sometimes it is as simple as adding a flip cap, as Colgate did in toothpaste (driving the point home in ads featuring Flip Wilson). VO5 shampoo became the best-looking brand of value hair-care products when its labels changed from paper to clear plastic. Gillette Dry Idea roll-on antiperspirant leveraged something as simple as a bigger roll-on ball.

Ivory shampoo and conditioner became a $100 million brand in year one largely via an innovative trial strategy. Rather than introduce the product with the salable sample sizes that were common at the time ($.69 for three ounces), P&G distributed high-value coupons. When consumers used the coupons on aggressively priced full-size bottles, they got a full-size product for the cost of a traditional sample. Retailers lined up for their "allocation" for this launch.

Don't let organizational divides get in the way of innovation. Often there is highly marketable "clay" in other divisions or countries just waiting for you to grab it, shape it, mold it, and launch it. Often this clay is two doors down. Pantene Pro V, now the world's leading hair-care brand, was built on the Pert Plus's shampoo-plus-conditioner technology applied against a radically different consumer message. This was the ultimate in search-and-reapply innovation.

Discontinuities: Exploiting the Creases

Another potential source of innovation is discontinuities. Our world is full of them. Somebody or something is constantly moving the cheese. Some of the discontinuities come upon us like a freak tornado (such as a new and truly superior competitive offering). These are typically the ones that are easy to get your organization to rally around. We can all see events, but most discontinuities creep up on us. It's hard to get perspective when your face is up against the glass.

A surprising number of leading brands and companies got their big break from the ultimate discontinuity: war. P&G cornered a key soap ingredient during the Civil War. The Great War (World War I) was a boon to companies like Gillette in razor blades. And the tobacco companies benefited hugely from the World War II military practice of including cigarettes in rations. Talk about a sampling opportunity.

You don't need social upheavals as dramatic as a war to relocate your brand, however. Value brands can make big leaps forward during the early parts of economic downturns (real or just perceived). Likewise, luxury brands can jump-start their growth during critical inflection points in an economic expansion. Exploit these cycles.

Technical changes in media have created numerous discontinuities seized by alert marketers. Brands like Ivory and

Beware of the Boiled Frog

The boiled-frog syndrome illustrates the stealth of discontinuity: Throw a frog in a pot of boiling water, and it will save itself by immediately jumping out. Put the frog in cool water and gradually heat the water to a boil, and the frog will let itself become a crispy critter.

Colgate were essentially created by the advent of national magazines a century ago. Radio created even more brands. Revlon is one of the many companies that were essentially born on TV. In Revlon's case, its live ads on game shows were supposed to be sixty seconds long but went on for far longer. (Who knew how to control these things back then?) Those ads made Revlon a household name in ways TV could never do today. Obviously, not all new media technologies are a boon to consumer marketers. The overreaction to the possibilities of the Internet has its roots in the collective memory of the first-mover advantages that getting on the TV bandwagon provided in the 1950s.

The microwave oven provided a huge discontinuity that companies like Pillsbury rushed to exploit. The driving need for convenience has also led to such opportunities as one-handed food (for eating while driving), liquid hand soaps, and "canless canned" cat food (Tender Vittles). The invention of the VCR created a multibillion-dollar packaged-entertainment industry, providing huge "repurposing profits" to companies like Disney and Viacom. More recently, DVDs are giving entertainment companies a second wind, although in this case at least, they are usually adding features, such as interviews with the directors.

The brutally competitive nature of the consumer product industry was in stark evidence when P&G fully exploited Unilever's use of fabric-destroying magnesium in its European detergent formulas. This competitive misstep created a market discontinuity that turned the normally publicity-shy P&G into a trash talker with a megaphone.

Pepsi's exploitation of the New Coke debacle is, of course, another good example of competition-created discontinuities. When your competitor hands you one of these on a silver platter, don't be shy. As Ray Kroc of McDonald's was reported to have said, "When your competition is drowning, stick a hose down his throat."

The government is constantly creating discontinuities that can be turned into opportunities. When the FDA got lax about regulating antiwrinkle and baldness claims in the late 1980s, even the most conservative companies had to respond to the aggressiveness of industry upstarts. A few years ago, changes in food-labeling regulations required that almost every single product in the grocery section be relabeled, creating a significant competitive advantage for companies that had invested in digital asset management systems (as well as for the vendors supplying them). The clean-air regulations passed by the Environmental Protection Agency (EPA) and the more stringent ones by the California Clean Air Resources Board made almost all aerosol products either more expensive, less efficacious, or both, opening up competitive windows for suppliers of alternate forms. Mennen Speed Stick got a new advantage over its more aerosol-driven arch rival, Right Guard. Similarly, Dep styling gel got a new advantage over rivals selling aerosol-driven hair spray.

Borrowing from Other Channels

Consumer product marketers are always looking upstream to see what's floating down Channel River. Over the years,

Think in Metaphors

Another way to stimulate marketing innovation is to use metaphorical thinking. Consciously changing your metaphorical filters as you work through a problem is arguably the single most productive thinking tool available. Use it and its lateral-thinking partner, the analogy, often. At a minimum, be conversant in the many metaphorical languages used on and around your brand. Remember, marketing communications is all about language.

Contact with ad agency creatives, anthropologists (used for in-depth, one-on-one qualitative research), ideation specialists, packaging designers, and other right-brain-oriented professionals is part of what makes consumer product marketing such a fascinating career. Metaphors and analogies intentionally abound among these people. They make a conscious effort to paint word pictures, to visualize one thing by referencing another, to conjure. An awkward package design is "horsey." A cluttered print ad is "busy." A big advertising idea has "legs." Learn from this orientation.

Then there is the sales force, a stronghold for war and sports metaphors. Even if you hate history and sports, you'll have to at least learn the rudiments of these two topics if you want to really connect with your sales force and/or brokers. "There is no I in team." "It's just a matter of blocking and tackling." "Putting third should give you the line." "It's time for a distribution blitz." Even the phrase "field sales force" is utterly martial. Of course, the marketing function has always had its share of war references. We launch new products with marketing campaigns. We drop coupons on the market.

The metaphor of the driver or pilot has been gaining in usage recently. The old business school references to "key performance indicators" have been rechristened simply "the dashboard." Nielsen and IRI (Information Resources, Inc.) report a sales "metric" (a very hot word) called velocity, so, of course, the term minimum flying speed *has been applied to the shelf take-away needed to maintain distribution. "Helicoptering up for the thirty-thousand-foot view" hovers on the edge of overuse.*

Overall, however, the metaphor of the living organism is the dominant metaphor of consumer marketing today. Biology is a rich field to draw from, as well as more accessible and therefore more managerially correct than allusions to wars and sports and race cars. It also fits well with our cultural focus on raising children. We seek to grow and nurture healthy brands and in fact tend to think of them as sentient beings with personalities, strengths, and developmental opportunities. We think of ourselves as being the head, literally, of the organizational body— with the eyes, ears, and brains necessary to plot a course and adapt to changes in the environment. When a company grows without grafting on an acquisition, we refer to its expansion as organic growth. Successful companies are adroit at finding their ecological niche. Try picturing

(continued)

your fiercest competitors (the companies and their brands) in biological terms. Next think of yourself as a real or evolved biological entity that can handle them. If you are big, stomp them out. If you are nearly the same size, try forming some alliances and hunt them down like a wolf pack. If you are tiny, leverage your ratlike cunning.

a lot of fertile, innovation-sparking silt has come down from class to mass. You don't need to go to Starbucks to get ultra-premium whole-bean coffees anymore. Folgers has them at Kroger. If you want breeder-endorsed or breeder-developed dog food, that's just down the aisle from Kibbles 'n Bits. Knock-offs of Bath & Body Works lotions and potions seem to be in every grocery store.

The problem is that a lot of the class-channel marketing techniques simply don't float downstream very well. The defining difference between class (prestige or specialty) and mass distribution channels is the level of service offered. The mass market is almost one hundred percent self-service. Not so in class. In the case of cosmetics brands distributed through department stores, the biggest marketing investment by far is in services. Salespeople are immaculately groomed and are at the ready to spray you with fragrances and give you expert advice on how to look like them. In reality, they are hard-to-regulate, commissioned sales reps with a great temptation to overclaim. They don't need to get the network and regulatory clearance that advertisers need for what they communicate.

For years, consumer product companies have tried to simulate service in the mass-channel environment, with very little success. This effort is understandable and even laudable, but so far the execution has been laughable. Noxell's (eventually P&G's) failed Clarion cosmetics brand invested hugely in at-shelf computer consultation devices. So have the hair color companies. And dozens of brand leaders such as Tylenol, Gillette, Kodak, McCormick, and Kraft have dutifully rolled out educational "stores within a store," only to take them down when they didn't work. The problem is there really isn't much that needs to be said about most consumer goods. Their simplicity is why they work in a self-service environment. How much service do you really need to figure out that first you lather and then you rinse that shampoo?

Another pitfall to watch out for in translating successes in class to successes in mass is the packaging. Prestige packaging graphics are often so recessive, so subtle they would be totally lost on the shelves of the self-service mass-market universe. Of course, much of the design community loves this subtlety. Whenever you start a new package design project, make sure you or one of your team takes your designers to some real mass-market and class store shelves to discuss the very different communication challenges.

Graphics aren't the only packaging pitfall to watch out for. Many class brands are too tall or wide to fit on normal shelves. Some have a center of gravity that just calls out for tipping over, and others are so tiny they'd be pilferage problems at mass. Sebastian has a hair spray that comes in a can that's over two feet tall. Sephora is full of minuscule products that would walk out the door at a Walgreens or CVS (in Sephora's case, as in duty-free shops, the "service" people also play a large role in preventing theft).

If you keep at it, you can find the sweet spot between prestige and traditional mass brands. The payoff for creating this hybrid, sometimes called "mass-stige," can be huge. In the case of Salon Selectives shampoo and conditioner, our key idea was to simulate the customized hair "prescription" that stylists provide via an innovative versioning system that abandoned the conventional dry/normal/oily approach to labeling hair types. We had four shampoo cleansing levels (1, 3, 5, and 7) and four conditioning types (Highlighting, Sheer, Protective, and Body Building). This allowed the consumer to self-prescribe (mix and match) based on his or her specific hair needs. We also beefed up our prestige credential by using the Helene Curtis name as a maker's mark. We used a fragrance (green apple) that consumers associate with salons. Finally, we picked a name, Salon Selectives, that literally named the claim.

When you just can't find the sweet spot, there is the option of simply acquiring a class brand and taking it to the masses. P&G recently did this with Iams pet food, which had previously been available only in specialty shops or through veterinarians. Be prepared for the fallout, however. The jilted specialty channel will immediately discontinue the traitor and start bad-mouthing it ("they watered it down") as part of their push for the replacement brand that has maintained its channel purity, that is, its exclusivity.

Once a brand has lost its "professional" endorsement and is available everywhere the standard brands are, it will need to come up with a new source of differentiation or die a gradual death. This is happening now to the once professionally distributed Vidal Sassoon brand, also owned by P&G. P&G has attempted to apply what it learned from its hair-care mistakes to its pet food strategy. As Iams falls out of favor in specialty pet food channels, P&G is reloading those channels with a previously tiny but still pure (exclusive) brand, Eukanuba.

The ideal is to master both the mass and the class channels with different brand names. Still, it can be risky to spread your resources so thin, unless you have a high degree of category focus. L'Oreal is the master of this class-and-mass strategy. The company stays tightly focused on beauty care (where its authentic Parisian credentials offer an inherent advantage) and completely segregates its class offerings from its mass products. Very few consumers realize that the product they pay $50 for at Bloomingdales under the Lancôme brand name (owned by L'Oreal) is essentially the same as what they could buy for $10 at Wal-Mart under the Plenitude brand name (also owned by L'Oreal).

Passion

To win in consumer marketing, you need more than leadership and innovation, you also need a whole lot of passion. You need to be an unbalanced fanatic who has so much passion for your brand that you literally dream about it. You need to have an intimate, personal relationship with it. That's what being a monomaniac with a mission means.

The need for passion is what led to the invention of the brand management system, in which a separate small team of marketing generalists is dedicated to each brand and charged with leading cross-functional teams on the brand's behalf. Since its invention some seventy years ago, the brand management system has weathered untold scorn from all quarters. Its inherent shortcomings include a huge gap between responsibility and formal authority, significant inefficiencies, and decision-making friction that naturally comes out of any matrix organizational design. Brand management also leads to a limited view that can suboptimize overall corporate resources. But even today, this much-lambasted system remains the worst way to manage a multi-brand consumer product company—except for every other approach that's been tried.

Eat the Dog Food

My first consumer marketing job was in the Pet Foods Division of Ralston Purina, now part of Nestlé. As you'd expect from a market leader, the Pet Foods Division as a whole had an incredible amount of pride and competitiveness. Adding to this pride and missionary zeal was an expensive piece of claims research the division had just completed, proving that pet ownership helps people live longer. Wow, this stuff matters! On top of that, a significant portion of pet owners really do anthropomorphize their pets to such an extent that they consider the pets full members of the family.

And, boy, did we care. When R&D came up with a dog food that reduced stool weights or a cat food that helped pass hairballs, there was genuine celebration. When purchasing came up with a big advance in grease-resistant paper (critical for keeping the pet food fresh), we forgot for the moment that GRP usually stands for gross rating point. On Checker Day (the beginning of the fiscal year, when every single headquarters employee went to the parking lot picnic wearing a checkerboard shirt), the CEO could get ovations for announcing gains of one-tenth of a share point. Of course, almost all of us became pet owners, even workaholic single guys living in studio apartments. But the true mark of the passionate marketing zealot at Purina was, yes, taste-testing the pet food. Almost everybody did it.

Over the twenty years since my pet food days, there have been many parallels to eating the pet food. Passionate marketers wade into their brands, all the way up to their necks. Working on a nonirritating antiperspirant for women? Guys, shave one armpit. Need to relate to the macho man? Women, subscribe to *Guns & Ammo* magazine. Want to know what a woman feels like when she just steps out of a salon? Get a perm as a hair model in a beauty show—and then walk through the crowd to let everyone feel how soft it is. Need to relate to being a redhead? Become one. Whatever it takes to develop empathy, understanding, sensitivity, do it.

Try to make your mind work like Velcro, a sticky surface that holds on to every useful idea. You can get much of what you need to know from formal marketing research.

But the genuine article, the bone-deep consumer under-standing, can come only from living in your consumer's shoes—or paws, as the case may be.

Raid the Cupboards

Passionate marketers are notorious for checking cupboards, pantries, and bathrooms at parties (it can be more reveal-ing than checking out someone's music or book collection). Doing store checks while on vacation has become a carica-ture of the consumer marketer—but it's an accurate one. How can you pass up the opportunity to go into that regional chain store that you'd otherwise never get into?

Even when you're not traveling, it's critical to get into at least three or four stores a week, just to stay current. Challenge yourself never to leave a store without noting or imagining something new. Shopping is one of your biggest opportunities to see around corners. Be curious. Feed the intuition machine sitting between your two ears. The cacophony of signals you will find inside any retail store forms a rich pattern, a specialized language you need to be fluent in. "Wasn't there a private-label version of this brand here last month?" "I didn't think they allowed shelf organizers here." "This line must be going to closeout." "I thought this was a double-coupon market." The shelf set for your category in your key power retailers is your Rosetta stone. Learn to decode it.

And here's a commonsense tip too few marketers adhere to: talk to consumers in the act of making a purchase decision. (If you're a man, you can make yourself less threatening by holding a can of infant formula.) Also talk to store employees as they stock the shelves. Whatever it takes, fully deploy yourself; you're all you've got.

By its very definition (sensing and serving the wants and needs of consumers), marketing is a near-24/7 job. Be alert to how *you* are marketed to. Force yourself into buying situations you normally wouldn't be in. For example, pick up the beer for a social gathering if you're a wine drinker, or vice versa. Try to figure out why you've used Crest or Colgate all your life. In other words, don't forget to get in touch with your very own, always available inner consumer.

Have an Ego Made of Teflon

Being passionate about your brand also helps make you resilient to the inevitable setbacks. At the same time that you need Velcro sensitivities to pick up ideas and empathize with your consumers, you need to have a bulletproof, Teflon-coated ego to defend yourself against the naysayers. You need to be able to take a lickin' and keep on tickin'. Some of your brand-building ideas will inevitably be dumb, undoable, or both. Many of your good ideas will never get a good hearing. Consumers will dump on your new-product concept or promotional ideas, management will take a pass on them, and/or your peers will subtly and not so subtly ridicule them.

There is an easy answer to this: have more ideas. When one idea or program doesn't work out, just say, "Next."

Keep pushing. Challenge yourself to find one more best solution. Fight cold water with lots of hot water.

In summary, having a lot of LIP—leadership, innovation, and passion—can't get you to the marketing Promised Land all by itself. But without it, you don't have a chance of getting there.

CMO Checkpoints

1. Work hard to set the very best, most appropriate direction possible for your brand. No one else can do it.
2. Remember, you communicate far less than you think you do. Repeat your brand direction as frequently and as concisely as you can.
3. Act as if you literally own your brand as its sole proprietor. Assume your kids go hungry if you don't win.
4. Don't neglect the basics of managerial excellence: planning, organizing, and controlling.
5. Grab for every possible source of innovation you can, and demand it from every function in your company.
6. Exploit marketplace discontinuities; they are happening all the time.
7. Use your passion to push past criticism and setbacks. Coat your ego in Teflon.

Marketing Research

M arketing research has a lead role in laying the foundations for the tasks involved in marketing consumer products. Its purpose is to discover consumer insights. In addition, marketing research provides support for making some of the hardest calls of marketing. Is this product ready for introduction? Is this copy really breaking through the clutter? These two roles, discovery and decision support, make marketing research one of the key tools in building strong brands.

What Do You Call It?

The nomenclature of marketing research is problematic. The function has long been called marketing *research, since*

(continued)

its primary customer or user was the marketing team, especially brand management. In the past ten years, the name has changed at some companies to market *research to reflect the fact that the sales function, driven by the rise of power retailers, is now a fully equal customer for research. The intention was to broaden the scope to the entire marketplace, not just the marketing function. Unfortunately, the term* market research *can be confused with the type of research conducted by Wall Street organizations. Also, many sales departments created their own research groups, variously called sales analysis, customer research, and the like. But few companies can afford the inevitable duplication of effort and headcount to completely split up the overall research function. At the same time, ad agencies have changed the name of their marketing research function to* planning. *Meanwhile, some manufacturers now call their marketing research function the* information function, *something that is easily confused with the information technology function (the computer systems group). Finally, some companies have tried names such as* consumer insight department, *but this leaves out the increasingly important function of generating retailer and competitive insights. To keep things simple, I use the term* marketing research *as the umbrella term for all of the above.*

Types of Marketing Research

Marketing research can be subdivided in several ways. It can, for instance, be segmented by task—whether it will be

Types of Research Classification and Examples

Method of Investigation	Origination	Qualitative — Discovery	Quantitative — Discovery	Quantitative — Decision
Self-Reported	Primary	Focus group One-on-one	Perception study Segmentation study Tracking study	Concept test Copy test Product test BASES test
Self-Reported	Secondary	Reader surveys Supplier data	Yankelovich trends Census data MRI survey	NA
Behavioral	Primary	Observational	NA	Test market
Behavioral	Secondary	Specialized	Scanner data Nielsen TV ratings	Scanner data

used for discovery or decision support. It can also be broken out by the origination of the research, meaning whether the researcher uses primary or secondary sources. Other ways to classify marketing research are by the method of investigation and the degree of rigor. The choices the researcher makes along each of these definitions result in a variety of possible research designs, such as the examples shown in the chart on page 29.

Classification by Method of Investigation

A key way to classify marketing research is by the method of investigation. The key methods are behavioral (tracking or observing what consumers do) and self-reported or self-expressed (asking consumers what they do or what their attitudes are). Behavioral research does not ask consumers what they want or need or do. It just records what they do. Scanner data is pure behavioral data. Observational research is a rapidly growing type of behavioral research. A good example of observational research is hiring anthropologists to observe what goes on in a beauty salon.

The second method of investigation is consumer self-reported or expressed information. Survey research, whether conducted in person, by phone, by mail, or online, is an important form of self-reported research.

Classification by Origination

Most marketing research comes from secondary sources. Secondary research is not specifically commissioned by the individual marketer. It is either free, such as much of the information available on the Web, or it's syndicated. The Yankelovich Monitor, for example, is a large annual consumer trend study that costs millions of dollars to conduct. Because many marketers across many product categories are interested in the broad trend data, Yankelovich is able to syndicate its research. Doing so brings the cost per marketer down to a reasonable level.

The largest form of secondary research is government census data. Almost every other piece of research directly or indirectly uses census data, if for no other purpose than to help identify representative samples to study. Large media-related surveys, such as those conducted by MRI, are another example of broadly used secondary research.

The sources mentioned so far are self-reported secondary data. Much secondary data is behavioral, however. Examples include syndicated store scanner data and Nielsen's passive TV audience measurement research.

Although most research data comes from secondary sources, consumer product research departments spend most of their person-hours on primary research. This is research *initiated* by the company. The strength of primary research is that it is brand- or category-specific, and the individual marketer has full control over its design and timing. Most focus groups and product testing fall in this area. So do perception studies and copy testing.

Classification by Degree of Rigor

The third way marketing research is classified is by degree of rigor, that is, qualitative (small-scale) research versus quantitative (large-scale) research. Qualitative research is relatively quick and relatively inexpensive, but the results are only directional. Because of this, you can't—or at least shouldn't—make major decisions based on the results. Sample sizes are small, almost always fewer than thirty respondents. You can't run statistics on qualitative research; it is meant only to give a better understanding of consumer attitudes and behaviors in given situations. Focus groups are a key example of qualitative research. In addition, R&D departments often do small-scale qualitative studies as part of their product development process.

Quantitative research is slower and more expensive than qualitative research, but you can run statistics on it. Typically taking the form of surveys, quantitative research seldom allows for in-depth probing of consumer attitudes or motivations. Sample sizes range from 200 for a simple product test to 1,500 for a detailed consumer perception study.

Matching Tools to Research Needs

As a marketer, your job is to match the available research tools to your business objective, budget, and time requirements. This takes an in-depth and subtle understanding of the strengths, weaknesses, and overall applicability of each kind of research. In many cases, you simply can't afford the research you want. Your ideal research plan wouldn't leave you enough marketing dollars to take action on the information you uncover. On the other hand, few things are worse than making major investments in marketing based on research that is superficial—merely directional—though inexpensive. At the same time you are balancing budget constraints against the need for information, there is always the risk that a major, expensive piece of research won't turn up anything new of value. The following sections provide specific dos and don'ts for adopting the most frequently used marketing research tools.

Challenges of Marketing Research

Marketing research, as a discipline and a craft, is making great progress. But there are also some chronic problems. First of all, consumers are less and less willing to participate in the proliferating number of studies that are conducted every year. Research burnout caused by research clutter is real. Even without burnout, consumers simply have less time to participate in studies than was once the case. The result is that research costs are going up much faster than most other input costs. The Internet is helping a lot, especially with concept testing. On the other hand, no one has perfected the art of online focus groups.

Another key challenge for marketing researchers is their almost total inability to provide quantitative data about the actual behavior of individual consumers. It's quite easy to get hard data on what type of household is

(continued)

buying your product. In many categories, such as cake mix, you can safely assume that only one member of the household is using the product. In other categories, such as snacks or shampoo, it's likely that several different household members are using different brands. This is a major problem since most media and other marketing tools are based on the demographics of individuals, not households. Self-reported data is usually based on individual responses, so it solves the problem of multiple household members. But we know there is a significant variance between what people say they do and what they actually do. The Holy Grail of marketing research—affordable, individual-based behavioral research—is just starting to come into being.

Qualitative Research

Focus groups and their kissin' cousins, one-on-ones and dyads or triads (fancy words for talking with two or three people at a time), are part of the bedrock of consumer product marketing. In fact, groups (as in "Let's do some groups") are probably the number one procedural export from consumer product marketing to the world at large. Almost every industry and function now does groups. Certainly, they have become a core part of the political process.

In general, groups and other variants of qualitative research are great. How can you not get at least a few nuggets from sitting in a cool, dark, M&M-stocked sanctuary behind a one-way mirror, listening with your team to the thoughts and feelings of real consumers? So do qualitative, with a few caveats in mind.

The first caveat is to make sure you have done your homework on what you want to talk with consumers about and in what setting. Use the process of agreeing to the moderator's discussion guide as a way to force closure on this. Your specific objectives will pretty much dictate the kind of qualitative research you do, although there is some flexibility here. Your objectives will also help you select the best possible professional moderator for your needs. For coming up with a well-rounded view of underlying category needs or overall brand perceptions, the interaction you get from consumers in full groups is usually the best kind of research you can conduct. Full groups—that is, with eight to ten people—are also the best way of getting relatively quick responses to a fairly large number of stimulus options, such as concepts or packaging designs. If you are trying to go in-depth on just a few things, however, especially advertising, I strongly recommend one-on-ones or mini groups.

The second caveat is simply to take everything consumers say with a huge grain of salt. You can't do your job without having an insane amount of passion for your brand and category. Normal consumers can't live their lives without relegating almost everything related to your brand to the bottom of their priority piles. Consumers are far more interested in how they are performing socially in a focus group (and in the $50 to $150 participation fee) than they are in what you are selling. Because consumers don't have a big interest in your brand or category, they don't have a lot to say, either. They don't care much, so, reasonably, they don't know much. You are literally panning for gold. One of the dirty little secrets of consumer product marketing is how much stamina it takes to keep your eyes and ears focused on the gold when there is so much verbal slag to go through.

The third caveat is that consumers sometimes lie. Some sort of prisoner-captor dynamic goes on in front of a one-way mirror and creates a true reality distortion zone. No matter how much the moderator protests that he or she doesn't work for the company sponsoring the groups, some consumers just have to be falsely positive so they don't hurt the moderator's feelings. Other consumers are falsely negative to make sure the whole world knows that life's not fair. One trick is to listen carefully to how group members introduce themselves, so you can establish the appropriate "content filter" for what they say.

The herd instinct is another powerful dynamic that distorts communication in focus groups. It is truly fascinating to see how an alpha respondent almost invariably pops up and then subtly bullies the rest of the group into submission, resignation, or passive aggression. Who becomes alpha has a lot to do with the composition of the group. Make sure you don't put one or two apples in a room full of oranges. I've seen what I'm sure are self-confident, outspoken male executives become the equivalent of seventh-graders with acne when thrown into a predominantly blue-collar group. Likewise, well-dressed, attractive, unmarried women, when put into groups skewed toward moms, become suddenly mute. Where respondents happen to sit also has a major impact on who becomes alpha. Very often the seat closest to the moderator becomes the power seat.

Some alpha behavior is desirable in that it makes everyone take the group seriously. Much of the excessive display of preening or dropping out can be avoided by careful respondent screening and through the selection of an experienced moderator. But sometimes you need to take action to see that the bull elephant gets an important phone call and doesn't return.

A fourth caveat is to make sure you manage what is happening on your side of the mirror as deliberately as you do the consumers' side. At least 50 percent of the value that consumer product companies derive from qualitative research is the interaction that goes on within the team watching from behind the mirror. Make sure you get the right people at each group. Set an example of active listening during key times, but work the room like crazy during breaks and other downtime. You've got the best and brightest from R&D, the ad agency, marketing research, design, and your marketing team focusing on the fundamental questions of your business. Consciously leverage the oddity of sitting in the dark, toadstool-like, for days at a time. Away from the hustle of daily business, you'll find that you begin to think differently. Try to minimize calls and E-mail.

Leverage the unwritten rule of wearing extracasual clothes. Stare at your faint reflection in the mirror. Doodle away. Don't forget about the gold mine between your own ears.

If something is turning out to be unproductive in the groups, work with your team to change it. If someone has a new idea that can be worked in, work it in. If you're just not satisfied with the way the moderator is asking a key question, open the door at the end of the session and walk in to the arena yourself.

The fifth caveat is to avoid becoming a catty ogre. In other words, keep your self-respect by being respectful of your respondents. There is something godlike in looking through a one-way (your way) mirror at "average" consum-

Marketing Researchers vs. Line Manager

Qualitative work occasionally makes your marketing research professionals exasperated, exasperating, or both. Brand people are constantly trying to get more from the research than is possible ("Can't we just throw in the six package designs at the end?"). Marketing researchers can sometimes come off as rigid to the point of not caring about moving the business ahead. Keep in mind that this is their turf but ultimately you are the line manager. Remind them of the 50 percent that takes place on your side of the glass. Listen hard to their points of view, leverage your relationship, and then make the call.

ers. Inevitably, a few respondents are so inarticulate or unattractive that you will be tempted to show off your sarcastic, rapier-like wit at their expense. Resist.

Make sure you hear from everyone on your team during the debriefing, which should be held immediately after the last group of the day or night. If critical people can't be at the groups, make sure they get an audiocassette and listen to it. After the groups, demand at least a short "key takeaway" note from everybody. Win the qualitative!

Quantitative Research

Quantitative research encompasses a large array of research objectives and methods. The following advice covers the objectives and methods that are most common.

Brand Perception Studies The most important question in marketing is, What's your brand's positioning? The best way to provide a consumer-based answer is to conduct a large-scale study of brand perception. Brand perception studies provide multidimensional perceptual maps of the category, including your brand's location on the map relative to its competition. They also provide ratings of brand image and define consumer segments. Although a lot of science is involved, ultimately the utility of these studies comes from many creative choices the researchers make. They need to translate the data into meaningful names and concepts. That's why this is one area where you need to invest heavily in getting the best talent on the job, even if you have to wait in line for a particular researcher to become available.

Out of perhaps a hundred image-rating statements that go into a study, only a handful of underlying, mathematically derived perceptual dimensions prove to be meaningful. In other words, most of the image-rating statements cluster together in a few bundles of ideas that form the basis for actual consumer discrimination. It's seldom very neat, except for the dimension of high/low price. At a minimum, you will see which brands consumers perceive to be most similar to your brand on the most important dimensions.

Often, the research report will identify an *ideal vector*. This is the mathematically derived position on the perceptual map that delivers the optimum array of benefits to that particular consumer segment. In addition to seeing where you currently are and which way you should move to get closer to this "ideal," you can see where you have portfolio gaps. These gaps can and should direct acquisition and/or new-product development work.

Most perception studies mathematically identify seven or eight distinct consumer segments based on differences in their ratings of brand and category attributes. Most of these segments are problematic, not because they're invalid but because they don't line up with the marketing tools, especially media delivery vehicles, available to you. For example, it's common for a premium brand to closely align with a consumer cluster of, say, "vivacious conformists." You may find out that these are the heaviest users and the ones most likely to buy your brand's next line extensions. But how do you target vivacious conformists? Also, keep in mind that perception studies have the highest risk of just confirming what you and your management team already know. Cynics will say you could have learned just as much by reading the package backs of the leading brands in the category.

The best time to conduct perception studies is when you enter or are thinking of entering a new category via a new product or an acquisition. At this point, your collective knowledge base and instincts aren't well refined. Also, if you are a dominant player, you need to repeat perception studies periodically, since even a small insight can yield big results.

Concept Testing One of the most critical milestones in marketing is getting a good concept score on a new-product or new-brand idea. This requires coming up with an idea that is meaningful, unique, believable, priced right, and doable from the standpoint of technology, timing, and cost. Generating concepts is one of the real heavy-lifting marketing tasks. Recognize that strong concepts ordinarily come only after a great deal of foundational work has taken place. You need to fully understand the category, your brand, the available technology, your cost structure, key consumer trends, retail customer requirements, and so on. More important, you need a spark of conceptual fire.

There is great pressure to inflate the results of concept testing by loading more ideas into the concept than can ever be effectively communicated in advertising. Don't fool yourself or your management. Constrain your verbiage to not much more than will appear on the front of the package, in a single-page ad, or in a fifteen-second commercial. And don't rig the system by testing only among an overly narrow target audience. Be careful with your pricing. Mass merchandisers sell for much less than drugstores and grocery stores in most instances. Either use a blended average price in your concept, or test both prices.

Product Testing A lot of product testing can and should be done in the lab or in very small-scale studies. Many companies use employees and or church groups for quick and dirty product evaluation. Having this affordable scale of testing is important since there are often many formula options to consider, in addition to such aesthetic cues as fragrance or flavor.

Full-scale product testing—the kind you do to make launch decisions—needs to be rigorously controlled. Make sure you conduct your testing in season, if yours is a seasonal product. Make sure the home-use period is long enough to turn up issues such as product buildup or taste fatigue. Test your product against the key competition on a blind (that is, unlabeled) basis. Recognize that the packaging structure is part of the product, so try to use the actual package form you will be marketing. Make sure you get retains, that is, leftover product samples that the researcher had but didn't give to consumers. This is important both to preserve confidentiality and to make sure you have exactly what the consumers are evaluating.

One of the most challenging product-testing decisions relates to changing a big-selling product that is no longer as good, on a blind basis, as its competition or as an alternative formula you have developed. This was and still is Coke's dilemma versus Pepsi. Certainly New Coke was better than original Coke on a blind basis. It may have beaten it on a branded basis, even among current users, as well. But even a 70/30 win on such a significant product leaves millions of consumers unhappy. Fortunately, most brands have more leeway to make changes. Tide has upgraded its formula dozens of times. Vaseline Intensive Care Lotion has recently, after years of debate, changed its flagship formula from the original distinctive yellow to a now-consumer-preferred white. But, in general, be very wary of changing

Packaging Impact on Product Performance

The marketing team on Finesse conditioner was able to upgrade the product's performance significantly without changing the product at all. All we did was reduce the size of the hole in the dispenser cap so consumers wouldn't use more than they should. This presented a classic business trade-off. The smaller hole reduced the product use-up rate, hardly a way to build market share. But it increased long-term loyalty to the brand. We shrunk the hole.

the formula of a large, well-established product unless you have dramatic wins with a new formula among heavy current users of the original formula.

Test Marketing Most test marketing in the consumer product arena is now done via laboratory test markets rather than in-store. Store tests are simply too costly and give away too much information to your competition. And lab tests have proved themselves to be quite accurate.

Laboratory test markets are simply concept tests that also include a product-test component. If respondents express interest in the concept, they are given product to take home and use for a couple of weeks. Then they are interviewed again to see if the product lived up to the claims made in the concept.

BASES, a division of Nielsen, is the leader in this type of testing. BASES provides normative data, that is, benchmarks from thousands of other studies, against which you can compare your scores. Another very useful aspect of BASES is that it forces you to think through all your key assumptions of the introduction, including awareness, distribution build, retailer merchandising, cannibalization, ad quality, and so on. BASES takes all these input assumptions and models them with the actual scores from its test to generate a first-year sales forecast that is uncannily accurate.

There are many caveats to keep in mind when using BASES or one of its laboratory test-market competitors. First, keep in mind that these services are expensive. Make sure not only that you have a good concept and a good product before you go to them, but also that your concept and product fit each other. If the product doesn't live up to the concept claim, you may achieve your goal for the first year's volume, since 70 to 90 percent of a consumer product's first-year sales come from trial. But over the long term, you'll find yourself trying to refill a leaky bucket, as the low repeat rate drains away the economics of the product.

You also need to be careful about how you adjust the first-year forecast from laboratory test markets to translate them into a financial forecast. The results only project consumption; they do not take your distribution pipeline into account. They don't include potential volume from warehouse clubs. And the beginning of year one in a laboratory test-market forecast does not line up with the start of your shipments; it begins when you assume you will have "significant" retail distribution of about 20 percent.

A final major caveat with BASES and its competitors is that they are still more accurate for entirely new brands than for the much more common line extensions. A major issue is what to put in the model relative to sales cannibalization of the base business. Remember that line extensions can eat into base-business consumer interest as well as retail merchandising support. Another key issue with line extensions is what to put in the model for assumed awareness. All line extensions have some ghost awareness—that is, some people think they are aware of them even before they exist. You need to work through complex assumptions about how much of your line extension media is truly incremental to the base brand's media plan. My advice is to run several scenarios using different sets of internally consistent assumptions on each of the main parameters (awareness, distribution, merchandising). And don't forget to get your sales team's input on these.

Syndicated Store and Panel Scanner Data

Consumer product marketing and sales departments have near infinite terabytes of Universal Product Code (UPC) data to wade through. This is the data generated each time a retail clerk swipes a product across a checkout scanner machine or each time a consumer participating in a panel swipes an electronic wand across a UPC at home. With enough time, you can pull out the sales per million dollars of all commodity volume (ACV) per stock-keeping unit (SKU) by key customer, by week, along with a few phone books of "causal" diagnostic data such as the presence or absence of a temporary price reduction. Or you can pull out the panel-based purchases per purchase occasion and repeats per repeater. It's easy to go data-dumb. Fortunately, with a little common sense, you can extract 80 percent of the value with about 20 percent of the effort and expense typically applied.

Recognize the Limitations of Store Scanner Data

The starting point of effectively using scanner data is to simply recognize its many, many limitations. It can shine a lot of light on certain well-defined issues. But don't make the mistake of looking for too many of the keys to your business under the scanner streetlights, just because they are there. Although the quality of basic store scanning data is solid, keep in mind what it doesn't provide. It no longer includes Wal-Mart. It has never included wholesale clubs, most of the fast-growing dollar stores, department stores, or specialty stores such as Bath & Body Works or Sally. It doesn't pick up product sold through direct-selling techniques, such as those from Amway, Mary Kay, and Avon. What it reports as distribution is not really distribution, since it only includes stores where the SKU was actually purchased/scanned in a given time period, regardless of actual on-shelf distribution. This significantly underreports actual on-shelf distribution for new items or low-turn items and is a source of much friction between sales and marketing departments. The sales velocity numbers are just never right—SKUs with low distribution end up having very high reported sales rates. Finally, the category definitions are often off unless you invest massive person-hours in correcting them and keeping them up to date. Take a careful look now at what they include and exclude from your current categories. You will likely find cases where someone totally unfamiliar with your business has made a coding error that significantly compromises even something as fundamental as category size.

In summary, scanner data represents the full reality of your business to about the same degree that TV sitcoms represent real life. For the rest of the picture, get into the stores, go to focus groups, do primary quantitative research, study your competition, be a tourist, read till your eyes hurt, and keep checking your friends' cupboards, showers, and laundry rooms.

Store Scanner Economics

Scanner data is expensive, as you'd expect from a duopoly. IRI and Nielsen are the only games in town (and Nielsen has a monopoly in Canada and several other countries). It's not unusual for a consumer product company to spend close to what it spends on R&D for these research services. You can cut this data tax down to size, however. Buy just the basics. Unless you are the category leader, don't waste your money on too much customer-specific data or too much data granularity, that is, microdetail. And negotiate hard. Remember, to firms like Nielsen and IRI, the incremental cost to provide the data they are already gathering is negligible.

Nielsen and IRI buy scanning data from retailers, clean it, and repackage it for sale to you. Disintermediation—dropping the middleman—is already happening. Many power retailers sell or even give away their scanning data, which they call point-of-sale (POS) data, directly to manufacturers. Wal-Mart's Retail Link is a very low cost way to get your consumption data on a near-real-time basis (versus waiting for the four-week syndicated reports that come out a week or two after the four-week period). Retail Link does not have competitive data, however, so it's not the complete answer . . . yet.

Regardless of how much scanner data you get, make sure you set up a system to portray the data visually. Ideally, you can graph several years of weekly sales, along with references to key events such as media advertising, coupon drops, and competitive activity. Unless you are managing a $300 million brand that can afford proprietary marketing mix modeling, this is still the best way to determine what works. In particular, look at the sales spikes that you can attribute solely to advertising, and then look closely at your related products to see if there is any advertising halo.

Panel-Based Scanner Data

Chances are, you don't need to invest heavily in the other key product of the syndicated data services, home panel data. This is data generated by about forty thousand consumers (for each service) who are paid to use a home scanning device on everything they bring into their homes that has a UPC, that is, a bar code. Home-scanned panel data is now the only way to find out not just your own sales at Wal-Mart (which is available directly from Wal-Mart), but also sales of your competitors there, and hence your market share.

Other than this new use, home panel data is a service without a lot of utility. Its most highly touted deliverable is its ability to help you understand the behavioral differences between heavy-buying households and light-buying households. The problem with this is that it's seldom actionable. There just aren't economically effective ways to reach the people so identified. A better bet is to mine for heavy users in your major customers' frequent-shopper programs. Grocers representing 80 percent of food ACV now have these.

Although tapping into these programs is costly, at least you have a direct way to influence heavy buyers once you find them.

Marketers also use panel data to help them identify broad marketing objectives such as trial, which is measured by household penetration, or loyalty, which is measured by share of requirements. But almost every brand ends up wanting to do both, and increase cross-category usage to

Advanced Scanner Data Analytics

Be circumspect about ever buying anything from the advanced analytic groups of IRI or Nielsen. They push this stuff hard because it's where they make their margins. The people in these groups are from Mensa-land and while their mathematical models may be beautiful, the insights you need are rarely there. You can invest $70,000 to $100,000 in a so-called market structure study to find out what you could figure out on your own with three or four store checks or just by talking with some sharp retail buyers or category managers. Or you can invest in a price elasticity study that will cost you more than the contemplated price increase will deliver in the first place. Good strides are being made in capturing more of the many variables to put into Nielsen's and IRI's models. Maybe someday they will get there. But meanwhile, the world remains just a little too messy to put into an equation.

boot. Even if one specific objective could be identified, again the problem is that the marketing instruments available are simply too blunt.

CMO Checkpoints

1. Marketing research has two key tasks. It helps you discover and track consumer insights, and it helps you make decisions on planned marketing initiatives.
2. Be fluent in all types of research: primary, secondary, self-reported, behavioral, qualitative, and quantitative.
3. Make sure you get the right people from your team at your focus groups and other qualitative sessions. Many of the insights come from your side of the one-way mirror.
4. Don't rig your concepts by putting more ideas in them than your advertising can communicate.
5. Recognize that mass-market media tools remain fairly blunt instruments. You can't target super-detailed consumer clusters.
6. Make sure your new product concepts and products fit and reinforce each other. That's the only way to ensure repeat rates high enough to sustain a business.
7. Be aware of the many limitations of syndicated scanner-based information, especially the considerable volume it does not capture. Lean into the use of retailer-provided scanner data.

Advertising Creative

Advertising creative is the seething vortex of consumer marketing. It is the most visible and tangible responsibility of any marketer. Advertising is a hugely important component of the brands consumers buy. More and more, it's central to what retailers choose to buy and promote as well. The key question on the mind of retailer buyers was once, "What's the deal?" Now these buyers are asking, "What's the ad?" In Hollywood, a film producer has been described as a dog with a script in its mouth. Similarly, a consumer marketer can be described as a dog with an ad in its mouth. Effective advertising creative is indeed job number one. You can't win in consumer marketing without winning in advertising.

You Need to Believe in the Power of Advertising

The one and only success criterion for advertising is immediate and sustained marketplace results. The encouraging fact is that recent scanner and split cable research has confirmed that powerful advertising creative can make an immediate and significant sales impact, even with modest media weights. I have personally experienced the almost perfect correlation between the quality of the advertising and the level of consumer sales via the weekly point-of-sale scanner data that major retailers now provide leading suppliers. It used to be argued that advertising should not be expected to make a short-term sales impact, that its contribution builds slowly over time. We now know it can and must do both.

Despite the hard data that proves strong advertising can dramatically increase sales and profits, most nonmarketers and even some marketers still have a guarded opinion of its efficacy. One of my prior CEOs referred to advertising as "chicken soup," meaning it probably helps a little and at least it won't hurt. Very few top executives think of advertising as an investment in the business in the same way they view hard capital assets. Certainly, given the amount of ineffective advertising that most companies try at one time or another, some skepticism is warranted. On the other hand, it's critical that the marketing leader never lose sight of the fact that when done right, advertising is the fuel in the furnace of every consumer-driven brand.

Breakthrough Creative

A great example of the power of advertising creative is the comparison of Secret and Sure antiperspirants, both from P&G. Ten years ago they each had about 9 percent market share. Both had good formulas and good advertising. Since then, Secret has consistently run powerful creative that taps into the insight that a woman perceives sweat differently than a man. Its share has grown by 50 percent. In contrast, Sure abandoned its famous "Raise your hand if you're sure" campaign and then ran one weak campaign after another. Its share has been sliced in half. Same technology. Same sales force. Different advertising. In 2002, Sure finally went back to "Raise your hand," but it may be too late.

The power of superior advertising creative was also clearly in evidence in the ibuprofen battle between American Home Products' Advil and Bristol-Myers's Nuprin. These brands were virtually identical in formulation and launch timing. Both were from big companies with expertise in the category. Advil was advertised as "Advanced medicine for pain," directly communicating an important consumer benefit in a way that played off the brand name. Nuprin, on the other hand, talked about "little yellow pills," a message that emphasized a meaningless attribute. Bristol-Myers also tried a strained reference to "nuking" pain with the phrase "Nupe it." Advil won the battle and the war hands down.

Strong Advertising Starts with a Strong Brand Positioning

More meetings are held, more E-mail written, and more caffeine consumed during the development of a brand positioning than at any other stage of the consumer marketing process. It is difficult, frustrating, essential, and never really completed to everyone's satisfaction, even your own. But creating and agreeing on a meaningful, differentiated, and deliverable brand positioning is the essential first act of successful consumer marketing. A good brand positioning establishes a blueprint from which to build all of your brand efforts. It encompasses not just advertising creative but also packaging design, new-product development, claims development, marketing/merchandising plans, pricing, and channel focus.

Your brand's positioning shouldn't change very often or very much. It should be the long-term strategic anchor that purposely limits your domain of acceptable initiative and concentrates your efforts on the activities that will magnify and solidify your brand's place in the target consumer's mind. It's your sounding board. Memorize it. Post it all over your work group. Make it your mantra. Even if you are not entirely happy with it, it will give you the organizational traction you need to begin heading in a positive direction.

How to Write a Strong Brand-Positioning Statement

A brand positioning is best described as the conceptual space a brand occupies inside the minds of its target consumers. Think of a three-dimensional grid with an x-, y-, and z-axis used to locate a single point. One axis is the consumer-defined product category or segment the brand competes in. Butter, furniture polish, and toothpaste are examples of product categories. The second axis spells out the consumer promise, sometimes referred to as the proposition. "Gets the red out," "squeezably soft," and "so effec-

---

Own Your Positioning

Tide competes in the laundry detergent product category. Its consumer proposition is superior cleaning, wrapped up in its long-standing slogan, "If it's gotta be clean, it's gotta be Tide." Tide's brand personality is authoritative, easy to relate to, and reliable. As the long-standing dominant brand with leadership technology and many other strengths, Tide doesn't need to be overly clever in its positioning. It has taken the high ground. To compete, other brands have been forced to redefine the product category, come up with a different product proposition, invent a different brand personality, or use some combination of two or all three of these. For a long time Wisk focused on the liquid portion of the category and the "ring around the collar" torture test. Cheer staked out the cold-water-cleaning arena. Surf focused on smell. Make sure you write out the positionings of all your key competitors to make sure your brand positioning is ownable.

---

tive you can even skip a day" are famous examples of consumer promises that have been turned into memorable advertising language. The final and equally strategic axis lays out the "affective" qualities of the brand—that is, the brand's personality or character. Is it, for example, nurturing, innovative, or approachable?

Consumer-Defined Category You may think you know what category you are in, but make sure you are looking at your brand from the consumer's frame of reference. Avoid locking your brand into the past by being overly conventional. At the same time, watch out for the trap of inventing a bogus segment just so you can claim to be number one. Start with how the syndicated research services (such as IRI and Nielsen) designate your category. If you can afford it, commission a scanner-based market structure study to examine how consumers actually buy products like yours. Explore your way down to the smallest subsegment that can possibly make sense and then up to the biggest sector.

For example, Mrs. Dash is a seasoning product that could be positioned narrowly as a simple salt substitute or more broadly as a flavor enhancer. Find out what segment or category nomenclature is used in other channels and other countries. Study the origins of the established segment names to find clues to alternatives. Coming up with an innovative product category definition could just require a shift from a Latin- or Greek-based word to an Anglo-Saxon-rooted one. Some day somebody is going to leverage

What Kind of Beverage?

The beverage business heavily emphasizes redefinition of product categories. When "diet beer" became "light beer," sales took off. Gatorade's massive success is largely attributable to its ability to convince consumers to buy into the idea of a specialized "sports drink." Its marketers are trying the same strategy again with their entry into the "fitness water" business.

You may need to try many alternatives to get it right. Zima has failed to create the clear-beer category even by calling itself a "clear malt beverage." Pepsi similarly failed to create "clear cola."

And sometimes, all you need to do is wait for the culture at large to catch up with your idea. Vanilla cola is a very old idea. But given the amount of cola burnout now in evidence, Coke's attempt with vanilla this time around may just work.

the fact that the word *shampoo* comes from the Hindi word for massage, of all things, to come up with a more appropriate frame-of-reference word. The old cream rinse category was revolutionized by S. C. Johnson's Agree, which changed the category nomenclature to *hair conditioner.* Styling "foams," which had failed for years, suddenly became a big segment when L'Oreal invented the descriptor *styling mousse.* The point is to systematically challenge the obvious, even in something as straightforward as deciding what category you are competing in.

Brand Proposition Getting agreement on the second axis, the brand proposition, is usually the most difficult step in developing a brand-positioning statement. Millions of dollars are spent in brainstorming and concept testing to help come up with and qualify these. The problem is that the most meaningful propositions are almost always the furthest from being unique. And, of course, the most distinctive propositions are almost always the least meaningful. If you are lucky enough to find the sweet spot that is both meaningful and unique, chances are its appeal is depressed by being unbelievable and/or undeliverable. Finally, even if you somehow come up with an idea that is meaningful, unique, and believable—with a product formulation that delivers on the proposition—chances are the costs will be too high to offer consumers a good price or value.

The difficulty of identifying a great brand proposition is compounded by the need to communicate not just what a brand will do for consumers but also the reason consumers should believe your brand can do it. In other words, most brand propositions need both a benefit and a reason to believe (RTB). To compound the difficulty, every product benefit ladders up—or leads step by step—to a consumer end benefit. Meanwhile, consumers want to know more detail behind your RTB; they want proof that it is real. L'Oreal's brand positioning consists of four "ladder rungs." The brand is created in Paris, the beauty capital of the world, so its marketers are credible when they claim to have superior beauty-care knowledge, so you can believe you will look good (or young) when you use the brand, so ultimately, you will feel you are a special person ("Because you're worth it").

The really hard part is choosing the one or, at most, two appropriate parts of this logic sequence to focus on. It's very difficult to communicate more than this, especially if the ideas are not fully linked—if the rungs on the ladder aren't in full alignment. In most functional categories, the chosen rungs tend to be the product benefit and the supporting attributes. In the claim that Zest cleans better because it rinses clean, "cleans better" is the product benefit, and "rinses clean" is the reason to believe. Product categories that are more image oriented tend to use only the consumer end benefit ("Brut makes you smell like a man"). But there are many permutations. Altoids make you feel like an interesting and attractive person because of their curiously strong flavor. Suave talks about the attribute of being less expensive, skips the product benefit (other than through a visualization), and focuses on the consumer end benefit ("Don't you look smart?"). Joy dishwashing liquid used to do the same thing: lemony ingredients that result in dishes that are "A nice reflection on you."

Brand Personality The third axis of brand positioning is the personality statement. The ideal brand personality statement consists of approximately three simple, declarative words that paint a picture of your brand. For most brands, one of these words will have an interpersonal or social aspect. Is the brand approachable or glamorous or down-to-earth? A second word will locate the brand along the dimension of time. Is it ultramodern/state-of-the-art, old-fashioned/classic, or simply contemporary? The third word attempts to personify the brand. Is it spirited, confident, or bold, for example?

When you are picking your personality words, mood boards full of scrap art torn from magazines are indispensable, as are competitive packaging and advertising. Go through the exercise of picking what kind of person, car, magazine, country, animal, store, or movie character your brand would be. Add enough texture to be sufficiently descriptive without adding so much that it becomes overly prescriptive. Sometimes it helps to write a back story about

The Power of Personality

BMW and Mercedes are both expensive German automobiles, but their personalities are completely different. BMW is exciting, young, and aggressive. Mercedes is accomplished, intelligent, and mature. Oldsmobile is dead because GM could not figure out how to give it a personality that was attractive but still different from sister car Buick. Most of the differentiation between Coke and Pepsi is based on their differing communication of youth.

what the brand would be like if it were a person. You can also think of this as representing what your idealized heavy user would be like.

You will never be able to get full agreement on the exact words to use in your personality statement. But once you have done your homework, your soul searching, and your mood-board work, you need to pick the words and make everyone use them consistently, year after year. I strongly recommend you come up with an acronym so you can remember them and make them a full part of your brand's strategic stump speech. On Finesse hair care, we used CAGE (pronounced *cagey*) for many years. It stood for captivating, approachably glamorous, and exciting. For another brand, we used FSI as a way to remember the personality of feminine, self-assured, and innovative.

Positioning Complex Brands

In the past, many brands had just one advertising message behind one advertised product. They were monobrands with monomessages. Today, most brands are more complex than this. For example, even a brand as basic as Olay has numerous advertised products, with different target consumers and consumer promises. There's Olay ProVital facial care that gets rid of age spots for women over fifty. There's Olay body wash for gently cleaning the skin of women of all ages. Now there's Ohm by Olay, a fragrance-driven collection for young women, inspired by the success of retailer Bath & Body Works. Thus, the marketer needs a total brand "highest common denominator" promise plus two or more individual product or target audience statements. In many cases, only the third positioning axis, the brand personality statement, applies to all advertising. You will need to work out separate category reference and brand proposition statements for each advertised product.

Translate Your Positioning Statement into a Creative Brief

Once you have identified the three axes of your positioning statement for your brand and its advertised parts, it's relatively easy to complete the ad agency document variously known as the creative strategy, the copy platform, or simply, the brief. Since you will have involved your agency fully in developing the positioning, they should be able to take the lead in this. All agencies have their own format for briefs, and it's usually advisable to allow them to use the one they're familiar with, rather than imposing your own. On the other hand, you do need to make sure they clearly include the core elements described previously.

Fully Leverage Your Advertising Agency

"Advertisers get the advertising they deserve." This is a chestnut for the ages, but it's largely true. You really can deserve highly compelling, successful advertising by mastering just a few of the fundamentals of working with your advertising agency. The very first thing you need to do is to create a situation-specific vision—or charter—of the kind of advertising you want. Be honest even as you are being ambitious. Not many brands should aspire to have "talked-about advertising," as Pepsi once did. Very few brands can even *think* about Nike-like advertising, where the talent fees could dwarf the media investments. Even within "normal" consumer product categories, very few brands can afford umbrella branding campaigns, which are designed primarily to communicate the brand image or core values or emotional connections of the overall brand, rather than to specifically sell hard benefits or launch new variants of an established brand. As simply as possible, identify and describe where your brand fits in the overall advertising food chain. Don't just make assertions. Back up your proposal with rationale and examples of success (without getting too hung up on history or competitors). Then get broad buy-in from top management, your marketing leadership team, and other key internal function heads.

Some people suggest that you can't create an advertising charter without major input from an agency. Certainly you should, at the right time, get the agency's input and listen hard. But you own the decision on what *kind* of advertising makes sense for your brand, just as you own the specific brand creative strategies. You are the line, corporate representative directly accountable for the productivity of the huge investments your company makes in advertising. Your stakeholders cannot afford to have the person in your role be a passive client. You need to be a proactive advertiser, with a well-thought-out and articulated point of view on what works for your situation.

If your advertising charter calls for the traditional and almost always appropriate emphasis on advertising that sells, rather than, say, advertising that will get your distributors excited, be ready for some extra efforts to get your creative teams motivated. Typical agency complaints about this orientation include the obsession with test scores (an issue that deserves to go away now that the creative testing methods have greatly improved) and the general grind of handling—with the required meticulous attention to detail—the sheer volume of assignments (TV and print, thirty- and fifteen-second options, new and nonnew versions, Spanish and French versions . . .). At the same time, agency management loves the stability of advertising-that-sells advertisers, their relative loyalty, and their bone-deep belief in the power of advertising.

Ad agencies also love advertisers who know what they want and who "give good brief." Even if your charter and creative strategies call for the agency to do what some of their (junior) creative teams will inevitably call "boring old hard-sell dross," they will tend to put many of their best and brightest on your business. But not enough of them. You have to be a nudge; a squeaky wheel; a consistent and persistent demander of excellence in all areas, including quality and quantity of people assigned to your business. Making the relationship click also requires that you market yourself and your brands to your agency or agencies. Go there. Cheerlead. Send flowers. Leave networkwide "attaboys" on their voice mail. Listen to them. Put them on a pedestal at your national sales meetings. Respect their work. Respect their time—and that means no Friday-afternoon creative meetings in Hooterburg. Learn how to do videoconferencing. Return their calls and E-mail messages. Do a good job of setting joint objectives. Give them the same kind of ongoing and formal performance feedback you give your top internal talent. Remind them of the centrality of advertising to your business. Hold out the (legitimate) carrot of new or incremental business. Help them get new clients. Be concerned with their profitability. And most of all, share your passion for the business.

Think of Your Agency Staff as Your Staff

The advertiser/agency partnership has always been important. The progress made in compensation approaches, away from media-based commissions and toward professional fees, is turning the partnership into an even more linked relationship. The commission compensation system has the merit of simplicity and built-in rewards for success (in the form of higher media billings), and you can and should use it in some situations—for example, when the financial tools and/or people are underdeveloped. However, your default mode should be fee-based compensation.

The biggest benefit of the fee-based compensation system is that it makes you, the advertiser, start to think of your agency staff as part of your direct-reporting marketing staff. (Their numbers are usually expressed as FTEs, short for full-time equivalents.) This is especially important since the amount you are indirectly paying for salary and benefits of this agency staff on your business often equals or exceeds your budget for internal administration and people. Just as the sales executives at your company look at their direct people budgets plus broker fees, consumer marketers need to look at total costs for all marketing people, regardless of which side of the advertising table the people are sitting on.

Once you start to get into your agency's expense books, you'll notice how costly top creative talent is. Their billing rate is high for the same reason on-camera talent fees are high: advertising creatives are rare and precious creatures, and you want your agency to be able to afford the best of them. Be proactive about which ones are assigned to your business. Court them. Study their reels or books. Interview each other. Have a time-efficient relationship beyond the big meetings. Get counsel from your top account manager, but also get the input of the chief creative officer and agency president. Be realistic about what percent of their time you will be able to afford. Make sacrifices elsewhere if you need to fund more creative time.

Never forget that the primary reason you hire an ad agency is to gain access to world-class advertising creative talent. If you have a very strong marketing research department, you may be able to live without some of the account-planning resources. Perhaps you can skinny back on some of those seldom-read media post-audits to fund more creative. And maybe you can live without two assistant brand managers on that new product. Said another way, win the agency staffing plan.

How to Manage the Creative Process

When all the preliminaries are completed and the right team is working against the right objectives and creative strategy/brand positioning, creative development has its best odds of success. But even with all the time and resources in the world, you just can't legislate innovation, which is what breakthrough advertising creative is. In most cases when the innovation just isn't coming, agency management will figure out things aren't clicking. They hate to delay the initial presentation of new work for self-respect and financial reasons (this is the time they put most, if not all, of their high-priced creative guns on an assignment). If they ask for an extra week or so, you need to give it to them. Another tipoff is when the night-before "it's gonna be fantastic" phone call is a little too breathless. Although the advertiser/client owes the agency a decision maker (someone who can say yes) at every major meeting, sometimes it makes sense to have a less formal "working session" with just the core brand and agency team to help focus or kickstart the work. Do what gets results.

Win Your Creative Presentation Meetings

Go into every agency creative presentation expecting to see home run after home run. We've all been overly trained to be great defect detectors, but you need to psyche yourself and your team up to see the big ideas when they are there, recognizing that most of them originally show up less than fully cooked. Get the best room, make sure the right people will be available, schedule the best morning time slot, get the coffee flowing, smile, nod, actively listen, take some notes—win the meeting. I've actually brought my personal checkbook to critical, high-tension creative presentation meetings to make sure everyone knew our objective and expectation was to buy what the agency had to sell there and then.

Scientists talk about Type 1 and Type 2 errors. One is accepting the false (saying yes to weak creative). The other is rejecting the true (saying no to high-potential creative). In other words, it can be just as wrong to say no as it sometimes is to say yes.

There are several meeting techniques you can use to improve your odds of getting great creative. A key tactic is simply to let the agency make the presentation with minimal interruption, other than nods of understanding or a quick question for clarification. Agencies rehearse their creative unveiling carefully, and you should take advantage of this. Whatever you do, don't get caught in a discussion between an inevitably defensive ad creative and a junior brand person on a board or script you aren't even interested in. Let the agency go through all the work twice while you quietly take a few notes (particularly on your initial gut reaction) and then insist on their making a recommendation. Make sure everyone is using the same name for each board instead of referring to "that third one from the end."

Then call a time out. Take a break. Depending on the amount of work and the size of your team, you may want to huddle without the agency in the room or bubble (that is, talk among yourselves with the agency present but not participating). When you give the agency your feedback, focus exclusively on what you can say something positive about, be it an entire board or a nugget from a board you otherwise don't want to pursue. Filter your reaction and comments through the sieve of the creative strategy and project objectives, of course, but also through your big idea gut-o-meter.

The great paradox we live with in advertising is the fact that the most interesting ideas tend to minimize strategic brand linkages whereas the most tightly brand-linked ideas tend to be less interesting. After all, we are usually talking about everyday consumables, not time travel services or even sunset cruises. The goal is to find that sweet spot where the big idea naturally comes out of the inherent drama of the brand itself. One of my early bosses had a great template for sifting through and finding the gold in creative presentations. First he asked, "What is the creative about?" (Is it on strategy and linked to the brand?) Then he asked, "Is it meaningful?" (Is it a big idea?). The maestro-marketer doesn't go to the next step until he or she has found an ad that can answer yes to both these questions.

Win the Morning After

Your job is far from over when the initial meeting adjourns. Spontaneous and short-term reactions are critical, but so are morning-after thoughts. Make sure you get color copies of the creative work to study first thing the next day. Show the work to others in your organization, including administrative people, junior marketing people who weren't at the meeting, people from other business functions, and your design team, for example. You will learn a lot just from hearing what comes out of your mouth as you present the work to others. Don't be a macho lone ranger about creative decisions. Advertising is a team sport. You need to both lead and listen well. But then close the loop with your agency and deliver one piece of written feedback within twenty-four hours. Although you need to bless this memo, it can be a great training task to have a relatively junior brand marketer write it.

Troubleshooting

More often than any of us would like, the creative work does not meet your agreed-to objectives. Some of it may be breakthrough but off strategy. Other work may be bang on strategically but dull, or it may have already been taken by a competitor. In these situations, focus on the elements of the work that are going in the right direction, rather than rubbing the agency's face in work you don't like. Be as clear as you can about what you feel is missing. If there is a piece of work the agency really has passion for, request that they keep it alive but focus their next round of work elsewhere. If their passion persists, consider some sort of cost-sharing arrangement to get it into testing. But in most cases, follow the two-meeting rule. If they bring it back a second time and you still have no heart for it, do the humane thing and shoot it dead.

Don't give up on your strategy just because the creative doesn't flow the first couple times out of the gate. If a simple do-over with the original creative team or teams doesn't help, the best move is often to re-immerse yourself and the team in the underlying consumer insights that drive your strategy. Review what has worked with consumers in the past—on your brand as well as competitors.

If your current creative team just isn't clicking, if you're not getting the results you need, take the lead in reconfiguring the situation. You are accountable. Whatever you do, never put all your eggs in one creative team's basket. Make sure you have multiple creative teams working on your business—even if your agency has to hire some freelancers or use some junior creatives. The competitive dynamic of using multiple teams reflects the competition your brand faces at

Execution Leading Strategy?

Very, very occasionally, an agency's big idea can and should influence your creative strategy, with much caution, of course. Bristol-Myers Squibb Corporation did not have "hairgasm" in its creative brief for Herbal Essences. But that ad campaign, originally a rip-off of Meg Ryan's fake-orgasm scene in the restaurant in When Harry Met Sally, *has created a billion-dollar behemoth out of thin air.*

shelf every day of the year. Good agencies are great at handling this. If you simply can't make this happen at your current agency, skim off some money and hire your own freelancer—but tell your agency and show them the work. Or if you are still managing International as a separate business unit, get another office of your agency working on the same assignment. Ideas are the coin of the marketing realm, and it's your job to make sure plenty of them are in circulation, particularly regarding advertising, your job number one.

Mastering the Art of Compelling Advertising

In-market results are the only true test of how compelling your advertising is. Either sales go up enough to yield an acceptable return on investment, or they don't. Because the consequences of error are so great, you simply can't air or place advertising before you have qualified it via quantitative research.

Advertising creative testing, or copy testing as it's still generally called, is the ulcer god for the marketing profession. Some marketers believe the results are rigged—and even half-seriously accuse respectable testing services like ASI or ARS of reporting bad scores so they can get some more business! Every person you run into somehow knows your latest copy-testing "score"—your boss, the sales director, the dry cleaner. The universal fib about these tests is that they are just used as an aid to judgment. That is seldom the case in the modern marketing world. More than anything, your copy-test score is your grade as a marketer. You have no option but to master the art of getting good copy-test scores. Fortunately, with the improvements in research design that have taken place since the mid-1990s, mastering the art of score getting now lines up very well with mastering the art of compelling advertising. The following suggestions will help you get better copy-test scores. More importantly, they will help you sell more of your brand.

1. Only salience sells. Salience, or brand differentiation, is, of course, the focus of your concept testing and your positioning work. If you can't find salience in your entire brand, chop it into advertisable chunks that do have salience. Be absolutely certain the most salient nuggets you have found actually make it into your creative work. Jergens Naturally Smooth Shave Minimizing Moisturizer promises you can "shave half as often." Papa John's pizzeria promises "better ingredients, better pizza." Bull's-eyes.

2. Keep it simple. Focus on very few ideas. Make sure you have tight synchronization between the audio and visual elements. Don't make the consumer work at taking in your message. A good approach is to focus the original creative work against the smallest creative unit you expect to use, such as a fifteen-second TV spot or a single-page print ad. This will force you to focus on just the essentials.

3. Grab your consumers by the lapels. If you don't get your prospects' attention, you have no chance of getting their business. Wendy's use of a little old lady asking, "Where's the beef?" broke through the commercial clutter so well that the slogan made it into the national vernacular.

4. Inextricably link your brand to the message. It's not enough to just get consumers' attention. You need to make sure they associate your brand with what they remember. It's called related recall. If not handled adroitly, the attention-getting element can be a brand sucker, a visual or audio vampire. Not only is AFLAC's use of the annoying duck a good attention-getting approach, it also links the brand name tightly to the message. Folgers's "Best part of waking up" jingle has the brand name right in it.

5. If you are lucky enough to inherit a brand with strong advertising equities, stick with them until you are sure your consumers (not you) are tired of them. Advertising equities can be jingles, characters, a distinctive look, a color, a product demonstration, a killer end-benefit visualization, or a slogan. Take the marketer's Hippocratic oath to first do no harm. Resist change for change's sake. New people want to make their mark. Sales may be flat (for a million reasons). But never underestimate the power of consistency.

6. Although some agency creatives squirm at the thought, make them sit through at least some of the presentation of the copy-test results. Push the copy-testing service to

Excellent Equities

If you don't have any long-standing advertising equities, it's your job to build some. The following examples belong in the advertising hall of fame: the Sprint pin drop, the Masterlock bullet shot, the Marlboro Man, Tony the Tiger, the Pillsbury Doughboy, the Tum-te-tum-tum sound bite for Tums, the Certs drop of retsin, the Lubriderm alligator, the Dove one-quarter cleansing cream line and visual, the Clinique package as hero, the renditions of the Absolut vodka bottle shape, the milk mustache, and the Trix rabbit.

bring in its most experienced people, who tend to be less dogmatic. The senior people at print-testing services tend to be especially insightful.

7. If you can afford it (or if you can negotiate a freebie), test some competitive creative that is driving the competitor's business.

8. Push your research supplier for more specific benchmarks to compare yourself to. Make sure they keep you up-to-date on the research they do on their own research, especially long-term case studies.

9. Don't just study the copy-testing numbers. Read the "verbatims." These are the unedited words real consumers use to describe what your advertising communicated to them. Although most research now comes

with some diagnostic numbers, there's no substitute for the actual language consumers use.

Reducing Costs in Advertising Production

The cost to produce an ad is one of the great sticker shocks of every new marketer. May the shock stay with you! Resistance is not futile.

Know Your Production Cost History

The first thing you need to do is simply study your own cost history. Make sure you know the actual total costs of everything your company has produced over the past several years. Your financial analysts will have a ball sinking their teeth into this project. Make sure they get the total costs, including talent, casting, music, and so on and that they show the data on an apples-to-apples basis. You will be surprised by how much the per-ad cost varies over time, even for the same brand. Go over these costs with your team in the context of the finished ads and the competitive set.

Get Your Agency's Production Team Involved Early

Have your agency's production department put together a presentation on how to save money on advertising production, using your specific history as a key part of it. Although it's true that the teacher often learns more than the student in these kinds of presentations, agency production professionals really do know the cost factors cold, as do most advertisers. The leverage is simply making the factors top-of-mind.

Once you have gone through this exercise, go the next step and jointly agree on next year's production budgets. And make sure the creative team knows about this going in. Although you can and should sidestep budgets when a truly big idea comes along, the team creating the advertising should know your expectations and not come in with boards that unnecessarily call for aerial shots or exotic location shoots.

Bundle Production

Bundling ad production is the single biggest thing you can do to reduce your per ad production costs. You can just take 25 to 35 percent right off the top. It takes planning. It creates some tension. But producing a one-off ad is at least a venial sin, if not a cardinal one. There are creative ways to bundle, too. Sometimes you can bundle across brands, although this is much harder than bundling across executions within a brand. Sometimes you can give a production company a multiproduction deal even if the ads are staggered over several months. Sometimes it's as simple as giving all the work—print, TV, and even collateral production—to the same production company, recognizing there are trade-offs relative to areas of specific expertise.

Plan Ahead

The second biggest step you can take to reduce your production costs is simply to plan for enough time to do it well without paying the excessive "rush charges." As you know from what happens internally when you rush a process (think sales samples), rushing advertising adds to costs exponentially. Sometimes you can solve the time problem just by factoring it into your media plans. For example, since print production inherently takes longer than TV production, you can plan to have TV be your kickoff medium. Or, recognizing that your objective is to have a fully integrated simulcast of your communication message in all media, you can buy weekly magazines rather than monthlies.

Target Brand-Appropriate Production Values

Avoid overspecifying your ad production. You don't need and can't afford A-level directors or photographers in most cases. Leave them to Lexus and Hollywood. This is especially true when the assignment is a simple pool-out— an ad that does no more than freshen up an existing campaign. Remember, A-level directors and photographers demand A-level crews, multiplying the cost. Seek out the rising stars.

Never Pay Retail

Don't pay retail. Negotiate everything. Challenge markups. Lower the cost of doing business with you (for example, go to the agency for the preproduction meeting). Leverage the agency's other clients' clout. Bring in a production consultant on an à la carte basis. In some cases, go back to the well and reboard the ad to round it down to a shoot lasting fewer days. Evaluate using the highest-cost talent to shoot just the principal photography while using lower-cost resources to shoot the packaging, for example.

Use On-Camera Talent Wisely

There are many ways to lower the cost of on-camera talent, although what you pay for this talent does pretty directly show up on the screen. Remember, you pay an incredible premium for on-camera talent that can act as well as look good. If you can get away with an off-camera voice-over, it will save you a lot. Don't put too many people in the ad. This will save you money and usually will improve the clarity and effectiveness of your ad. Use hand models and other specialist models if you can. And look very hard at out-of-country production, where you can often save hundreds of thousands of dollars on talent residual payments, even if the actual shoot costs are a bit higher. We once saved more than

Be Careful About Superstar Talent

Be very careful about hiring stars. I once had the pleasure of shooting a commercial with Sharon Stone, who was an exemplary professional and a big help to Finesse shampoo. However, I've also had the experience of supermodels showing up to the set not only hungover and puffy-eyed but with disruptive rock star boyfriends in tow.

$500,000 on a Salon Selectives ad by shooting it in Australia. Canada also has great production resources.

Make Sure You Really Need New Production

Make sure you absolutely need new advertising in the first place. Sometimes you can refresh or re-edit or adapt your old ads. Or just keep running them as-is. Get creative with the magazines and programs you advertise in to find new, underexposed target consumers. In other words, treat every ad production dollar you spend as nonworking overhead that you need to minimize. Again, you and your total team need to think of each dollar spent as your money.

CMO Checkpoints

1. To win in consumer marketing, you need to win in advertising.
2. Strong advertising starts with a strong brand positioning.
3. Be creative in determining your brand's category definition, consumer proposition, and personality (the three axes of a brand positioning).
4. Sell yourself and your brand to your ad agency.
5. Think of the agency as being on your payroll.
6. Take advantage of the insights copy testing provides.
7. Don't pay retail for advertising production.

Media

Media is the Rodney Dangerfield of marketing; it gets no respect. The pay scales are lower than in any other ad agency function. The media department is usually the last one invited to agency new-business pitches. Aspiring account execs typically start out in media-planning boot camp before being "promoted" to entry-level account jobs. On the advertiser/client side, media is the area of marketing that top management pays the least attention to. Even if the advertiser is big enough to have its own media people, they are invariably on the strategic sidelines.

This lack of respect just shouldn't be. At most consumer companies (as opposed to business-to-business companies), the dollar investment in advertising media dwarfs any other single expense area in the entire company. Media dollars expressed as a proportion of total sales range from 5 percent for the typical food manufacturer, consumer bank, or apparel company to 30 or even 40 percent in cosmetics, fragrances, and some entertainment sectors. These kinds of dollars alone should get the media function a whole lot of respect and mental investment.

Media is also important because it is changing so fast in so many ways, creating both opportunities for the astute marketer and traps for those who are less alert than they should be. The growth of cable and satellite TV, the adoption of time-shifting technologies such as VCRs and TiVo, and the explosion of the Internet and video games are just a few of the more visible changes. Other changes include the massive global consolidation of media companies, the gradual merging of advertising with news or editorial, the abolition of the once-adhered-to magazine rate card, and of course, the quantum increase in the sheer volume of media-delivered messages.

The only reason I can think of for why media gets less than its fair share of senior-level attention is that it is so hard to evaluate it objectively. As imperfect as copy testing or product testing is, at least you get a score. The only score media people are ever judged on is cost changes. And even here, there are no accepted points of comparison. Not once have I heard a senior manager attribute business results, positive or negative, to the quality of the media plan itself. But just because something is difficult to measure, that doesn't mean it's not critically important. In fact, media is one of the highest-leverage areas for you to focus on if you are committed to winning in the marketplace.

ABCs of Advertising Media

Advertising media is the pipeline through which your messages reach consumers. You can think of traditional mass media—such as network television or newspaper advertising—as a one-way pipeline. They deliver messages to a broad-based audience of viewers or readers. Other media, like cable TV, specialty magazines, radio, or targeted direct mail, are narrower, reaching audiences segmented according to special interests. Communications still flow in one direction, from advertiser to consumer. Interactive media, such as Internet sites, chat rooms, or E-mail newsletters, allow for two-way communications. Information is able to flow from the advertiser to the consumer and back again. Picking and managing the appropriate pipelines is a major part of every consumer marketer's job.

The sheer number of messages consumers receive on a daily, even hourly basis represents the biggest challenge for

Mass Media Still Dominates

The focus of this chapter is traditional mass media, especially TV and magazines, which continue to account for more than 95 percent of media budgets for consumer products. Interactive media is addressed in the final chapter, in the context of the future of consumer marketing.

marketers when it comes to selecting appropriate media. Consumers are bombarded by advertisers, not only when they switch on the TV, but when they pick up a newspaper, tune in their favorite radio stations, catch sight of billboards as they speed down the highway, sort through their mail, or browse the Internet. As an advertiser, you need to find out which media will push your brand into the consumers' consciousness. You might need to bang on the front door with a prime-time TV campaign, sneak through the window with teaser ads in your target buyer's favorite magazine, or pick the lock with interactive communications on your Web site.

How to Set Your Media Budget

Deciding how much to spend on media for your brand or brands is an act of triangulation and triage. First, there is no single best way to arrive at a final media budget, so you need to combine several approaches. Second, there is never enough money to go around—this is where triage comes in. And turf wars are a fact of life when it comes to divvying up tight marketing dollars.

Before you even think about how much to spend on media, make sure that advertising is the best possible investment you can make. In other words, you need to determine the role of advertising in your brand's overall marketing mix. The key is to spend to strength. That is, if your creative is weak, you will often be better off delaying a full-fledged media campaign, directing your funds to creative development, trade spending, or couponing instead. And if you have an innovative new product or an upgrade to a current product, a comprehensive sampling program might be a better investment than media advertising. Before rolling out its spot-TV and print campaign, PJ Squares—makers of prewrapped peanut-butter-and-jelly singles—sampled its new product extensively in grocery stores across fifteen states.

Let's assume that there is evidence that your brand is media responsive and you are convinced that you have compelling advertising creative. There are three methods you can use to come up with a budget that will meet your needs:

1. **The benchmark method**—How much do I need to be competitive?
2. **The task method**—How much do I need to achieve my communication goals?
3. **The pragmatic method**—How much should be earmarked for media, once all costs, profit requirements, creative quality, and priorities have been factored in?

Benchmark Method

The benchmark method allows you to draw comparisons between your own media spending and that of competing brands. Begin with a careful study of your brand's advertising history. Find out what worked—and what didn't work—in past media campaigns. To do this thoroughly, you need complete data on previous media plans: financial details, market shares, creative executions, copy test scores, and information on the competitive environment. Then, do the same thing—or as close as you can get—for competing brands. As well as you can, estimate the annual media spending of each of your competitors.

When comparing your media spending and market shares with those of rival brands, avoid these three common pitfalls:

1. Don't believe everything media-tracking services tell you. Tracking services typically overstate spending by at least 25 percent. This is because they rely on standard media rate cards, which are charged only to the smallest advertisers. The final cost paid typically reflects deep discounts; the bigger the advertiser's clout, the deeper the discount. Compare your actual media spending with the estimates provided by tracking services to come up with an adjustment factor. From there, it's easy to figure out how much competing brands really spend.

2. Remember that syndicated scanner does not reflect total sales. Compare scanner data on your own brands with internal sales report figures to see just how far syndicates services fall short. Adjust competitive scanner data accordingly to estimate total sales.

3. As will be discussed in detail in a later chapter, Lesson 6, keep in mind that retailers often accept extremely low margins on leadership brands in big categories. You

Club Clout

The two huge wholesale clubs—Costco and Sam's Club—have never provided scanner data. This is a big issue in some categories. Clubs carry a very limited assortment of brands—typically two or three per category. For category-leading brands, clubs can account for up to 30 percent of annual sales, whereas they contribute nothing to second-tier brands. Fortunately, the smallest club, B.J.'s, does provide scanner data. Use this information as a rough surrogate for total club channel market share.

need to factor this in when converting retail sales to manufacturer factory sales.

Once you have collected as much comparative information as you can on your brand versus competing brands, translate the data into the following three simple figures:

1. Total media spending per year
2. Advertising-to-sales ratio (A/S)
3. Ratio for share of category advertising spending to share of market (SOS/SOM)

By comparing past spending and proposed spending with your best estimates of spending on competing brands, the

> *Advertising-driven brands typically have SOS/SOM ratios greater than one, whereas "value" brands will have SOS/SOM ratios near zero. Dominant brands, even those driven by advertising, typically don't need to spend at the rate of challenger brands. This is one of the privileges of leadership. New brands often invest more in advertising than they get back in sales, resulting in SOS/SOM ratios as high as five.*

benchmark method allows you to decide how much you need to invest in media advertising in order to stay competitive.

Task Method

The task method of determining a media budget begins with establishing your communication goals. From there you figure out how much it will cost to achieve the goals. This is the high ground. Increased brand awareness is the key objective of almost every marketing plan. Almost every media agency has a general model that will tell you how many annual target rating points or impressions it will take for you to reach that goal. Some marketers try to establish more specific goals—or at least rules of thumb—such as the number of weeks or months they need to advertise and at what level. Giant brands invest in expensive marketing mix modeling—hypercharged number crunching—to get even more specific.

The importance of the task method is that it helps you establish a media delivery target that is based on your individual brand's marketplace dynamics, rather than relying solely on competitive benchmarks. It also gives you a standard of media delivery, irrespective of the ever-inflating costs of media. Because of this, the task method almost always generates a spending level far higher than you can afford. Still, it's helpful to know the ideal scenario.

Pragmatic Method

The pragmatic method for setting media budgets is the one that is actually used in almost all cases. It takes the ideal spending levels generated by the two other methods and adds them to the many nonmedia considerations all marketers deal with:

- What's available after covering product and fixed costs, profit requirements, and must-have trade allowances
- The management team's collective sense of the quality of a given brand's advertising creative
- The role of the given brand during that particular budget cycle, which is heavily influenced by the presence or absence of exciting new-product launches
- The presence or absence of new competitive threats
- The brand's strategic value to the company overall. (For example, a brand that has been deemed a core global

brand will get more media funding than a purely local one.)

Once you have established your total media budget, it's time to move on to more detailed media planning. By working smartly with your media planning and buying partners, you can significantly enhance the impact of any plan, regardless of spending level.

Media Selection: Know Thy Target Audience

Picking the appropriate consumers to target your media impressions against is critically important. This is surprisingly difficult to do, but it's well worth the effort. The data sources for making even the elementary demographic determinations are weak and often contradictory. The syndicated research services that media planners use, such as MRI, are based on the reported, not actual, behavior of individuals. And since the research questionnaires on which results are based cover hundreds of categories, the issue of respondent burnout is real. On top of that, the sample size of respondents for a specific segment is often quite small. The other major source of targeting data is behavior-based panel data that captures actual scanned purchases. The problem is that it is based on households, not individuals.

It often takes (expensive) proprietary research to fully answer the demographic target question. These custom studies are the best way to probe more deeply than mere demographics (age, gender, income, race, marital status, occupation) to the next level of targeting: psychographics (mind-sets, lifestyles, and attitudes).

If you don't have the money for custom research or even panel data, you can get a lot of information simply by systematically examining what your bigger competitors are doing. Media competitive analyses are often more important and insightful than creative competitive analyses because they bring to light something that is otherwise almost invisible. I'm referring not to the spending but to the specific programs, magazines, and other media the competition is buying.

Even if you have all of the relevant media targeting information, the decision of how to craft the plan is still far from easy. You will next need to grapple with the issue of how tightly to target your target. The problem starts with the targetability of the media universe itself. Even the most targeted general media available reach a high percentage of people outside the target audience. This is called spill or waste. Then there is the cost. Tight targeting is very, very expensive. The prime-time TV cost per thousand (CPM) to reach even a slightly targeted audience (say, women eighteen to thirty-four) is twice as expensive as reaching the slightly broader consumer target of women eighteen to forty-nine. Meanwhile, even a media schedule bought to the eighteen- to thirty-four-year-old target overdelivers impressions to women forty-nine and older, since they watch more TV in general. Steering media is like driving a bus—it's not rack and pinion.

Media planners and buyers are getting better at identifying the specific TV shows that the bull's-eye of your target has the most affinity with. You should fight hard for these. A big problem here, however, is that media companies are set up to sell packages, not individual shows. To get reasonable overall rates, you will need to accept some shows that are less appropriate for your target.

One of the best ways to improve your targeting ability without paying exorbitant premiums is to fully discard the need to be on individual shows with high viewership ratings. Few advertisers need to be on NBC's "Friends," let alone something as ego-besotted as the Super Bowl. Buying ten shows with a rating of one is just as effective as buying one show with a rating of ten, but costs a lot less.

What's important in TV buying is the total of the rating points you get rather than the number of shows it takes you to get those rating points. This is one of the reasons TV advertising—with its one-of-a-kind combination of sight, sound, and motion—continues to dominate consumer advertising despite the decline of average show ratings. The fragmentation of TV viewership has actually helped rather than hindered marketers. Cable TV should be a big part of your plan. It may take your media agency a few more phone calls to buy, but the result is better targeting and costs lower than for viewership concentrated in a handful of shows. The only people who should care about the declining audience share of the Big Three networks are the people at the (once) Big Three networks.

Fix the Mix

Once you have determined media budget and target audience, the next media decision you need to make is the spending mix among various media options. Will you blow your budget on network TV advertising or go for half TV and half print ads? If you have a small budget relative to competitors, it's often best to focus on a single medium. That way, you avoid costs of developing parallel creative campaigns for print and broadcast. If your budget is huge, it's wise to diversify and avoid oversaturation of a single medium.

Keep Options Open

When it's time to fix your mix, consider the following principles:

- For your product category, look at the norms and trends in the media mix for each brand, especially those of close competitors. As noted earlier, keep in mind that competitive data sources are far from perfect. While you shouldn't be a slave to the norms, it's wise to tread carefully if you are trying out something new.
- Be honest about the relative strength of your creative, and let it influence your decision. If you've got killer print

creative and only so-so TV, seriously consider going one hundred percent print.

- Be mindful of the issue of lead times. TV is a faster medium than print, and radio is even faster. If you think you may be late in developing creative for a new-product launch, it may be best to avoid the longer lead times that print requires. If financial flexibility is an issue—as it often is at year-end—that's another reason to avoid vehicles with long lead times.

Will It Play in Kansas?

Almost all brands and categories sell better in some areas of the country than in others. Sales of hair spray skew to the south. Body lotions sell best in the Rockies. As a part of marketing's due diligence, you need to be fully aware of regional biases. But also keep in mind the limitations on the data and the action set available to you.

The scanner services report market-by-market sales skews as Brand Development Indices (BDIs) and Category Development Indices (CDIs). Unfortunately, this data is only available for the grocery class of trade. For drugstores, Kmart, and Target, you can only get crude regional data. In the past, when grocery stores dominated consumer product sales, marketers put together elaborate plans that were very different for high-BDI/high-CDI markets versus low-BDI/high-CDI markets, for example.

Today, grocery stores account for only a minority of sales in most categories—remember, Wal-Mart is number one in food sales, too—so the available data needs to be taken with a large grain of salt.

Before you get too bogged down in minute regional analysis, decide what you are going to do about such variances. For most brands, the answer is "nothing." The reason is that local or regional advertising is simply too expensive to consider for national brands. For example, spot TV costs, on average, 60 percent more per rating point or impression than network advertising.

Consider, too, that the networks do not even come close to delivering rating points or impressions evenly across the nation. Networks chronically underdeliver in such key markets as Los Angeles and San Francisco while overdelivering in smaller markets like Milwaukee or Buffalo. But since L.A. and San Francisco are two of the most expensive markets in which to buy spot TV, regional buying is hardly the answer.

If you do decide that you simply must do some regional tailoring to your media spending, look for alternatives to spot TV. Outdoor advertising might work for you, or spot radio. If you are lucky enough to have a sister brand that skews toward the broad regions you're weak in, you can take advantage of a little-known phenomenon called network feeds. *In network feeds, ABC, CBS, and NBC allow you to split up the country into four*

(continued)

or five regions (depending on the network), and you pay national advertising rates rather than spot rates for each region reached.

- If your new product has good publicity potential, shift a portion of the budget into news-related media. Make no mistake about it, advertising spending influences editorial coverage. This is true for movies on late-night talk shows, and it's true for beauty-care products in fashion magazines.
- Leverage the media clout of your company. If other brands in your company's portfolio are using, say, transit advertising, chances are you can get some good pricing on your brand.

Consider Seasonality

If your brand is also seasonal—and sales of most brands vary at least a little according to season—you will need to decide how best to time your advertising to maximize exposure. What percent of your budget should you spend during a particular season? When should you start? Start too soon, and consumers won't be ready to buy. Start too late, and rival brands may snatch your best prospects. The unpredictability of the weather, too, affects your planning. While there are specialized services that will, for a fat fee, help you improve your weather-forecasting ability, these are worthwhile for only the most weather-sensitive brands.

Media costs, particularly the costs of TV advertising, also are seasonal. The cost of advertising on the networks, for instance, can swing by as much as 20 to 30 percent, depending on the time of year. Most brands don't take enough advantage of these cost swings. Media clutter, too, varies by time of year. Beauty magazines, for example, are as thick as phone books in September as the apparel marketers make their big fall splash. If your business is less fashion driven, you should avoid September, especially since your ad is likely to show up on page 450 or so.

Leverage Unit Size

Another important media decision is the size of each message unit you buy. In print advertising, think carefully before you decide, for instance, between a two-page spread or a single-page ad. As always, you should give heavy weight to the quality of the creative developed for each unit size. Also take into account the overall budget level and competitive landscape. The same consideration applies to TV advertising: do you need a thirty-second spot, or will a fifteen-second spot do the trick?

Reaching Consumers at the Right Time

The perennial media-scheduling question revolves around the tension between the desire to have a continuous media presence and the desire to be on big when you're on. The traditional rule of thumb was that consumers don't "go decisional" until they've seen your ad at least three times within an average category purchase cycle. This assumption led to the measurement of effective rating points (ERPs) and effective reach, which count a consumer as having been reached only after he or she has been exposed to your ad three or more times. This rule of thumb is now obsolete.

We now know you can greatly improve the power of your media plan by fully embracing the incontestable evi-

Don't Take Rating Points at Face Value

Rating points are used in media planning to measure two factors: the share of audience your advertising is reaching and the frequency with which your ad is reaching it. Ratings points are calculated using a simple formula: R × F = P, where R stands for reach, F for frequency, and P for ratings points. For instance, if you reach 50 percent of your audience an average of 4 times, then you have delivered 200 ratings points (50 × 4 = 200). If you reach 10 percent of your audience an average of 20 times, you've also delivered 200 ratings points (10 × 20 = 200).

The problem with ratings points is that they are rather like snowflakes—no two are alike. Not only are no two reaches alike, but no two frequencies are alike. Both the viewer who watches advertisements avidly and the viewer who clicks to other channels during commercials are included in a TV program's reach. The viewer does not even have to be in the same room as the TV in order to be counted. Advertisers have tried to compensate for the differences among viewers by creating a viewership index in which prime-time scores 100 while less attention-commanding day parts score only 50. Advertisers, too, have tried to mitigate the problem by awarding more points to thirty-second ads than to fifteen-second spots, on the premise that viewers are more likely to be exposed during longer units. Frequency, too, is not a fixed measure. A plan that delivers frequency very sparsely among a large number of people will have a significantly different impact than a plan that delivers very high frequency among a much narrower group.

Keep in mind that media measurement is far from being a precise science. By all means, use ratings points as a general guide. But don't make the mistake of basing scheduling decisions on them alone.

dence that just one exposure to a good ad can make a target consumer go buy the advertised brand. This approach to media planning is most often called the recency approach. The premise of the recency approach is that consumers are most influenced by ads they have seen most recently. Since you never know when an individual consumer will be in a store making a purchase decision, you need to maximize the number of weeks you're on air. Home-based scanner data combined with split cable advertising has proved that this is so.

TV and Print Picks

Once you've addressed all the big-picture issues discussed so far, you're ready to get down to picking your specific media vehicles—that is, the shows, newspapers, billboards, magazines, or Web sites that will carry your advertising. For TV, this means aiming for shows that your target audience has the most affinity with. Consumers are much more likely to pay attention to your message if it is embedded in a program they enjoy watching, rather than one that is playing in the background while they eat dinner in the next room.

Omnicom's DDB ad agency has long been a strong proponent of *aperture planning*, the objective of which is to schedule advertising so that it reaches your target audience at the time and place at which they are most likely to be making purchase decisions. A classic example is the scheduling of radio spots for Campbell's soup to hit the air as soon as temperatures drop below a certain point. Chap Stick ads on ski lifts are another good example of aperture planning. The advertising of breakfast cereals during early-morning news shows or before-school children's programming demonstrates that aperture planning can work just as effectively with nonseasonal, nonregional brands.

When selecting magazines, price per placement is just one consideration. You will also look at the following criteria:

- **Audience composition**—Go with the magazines (or books, as they are known in the ad trade) read by the highest proportion of people in your target audience. Studying the editorial will give you a good idea of readership, and so will the media pack that each magazine sends you.

- **Pass-along rates**—Consider not just the paid circulation, but the pass-along readership of each book. Highly produced, specialized, or costly books like *Martha Stewart Living* or *Bon Appétit* generally have better pass-along value than lower-cost, throwaway magazines. Take advantage of the "free" readers you're reaching through pass-alongs.
- **Magazine loyalty**—Look at each book's subscription-renewal rates as an indicator of loyalty. Determine also the ratio of subscriptions to newsstand sales.
- **Geographical coverage**—Compare each magazine's circulation with the regional bias of your brand.

Making the Buys

Buying media space and time is not much different from other buyer-seller situations. You'll see every trick in the book, as sellers try to up the price and you and your agency work to bring it down. You'll hear that demand is high, the economy is heating up, or that some high-rolling big spenders are pushing up prices. If the Olympics are on or it's an election year, you'll be told to be happy that you can get any space at all. If network ratings are down, you'll hear that space is scarce. A typical excuse is that make-goods—

free ads to make up for programs that underdelivered—are crowding out schedules.

On the print side, the wild card is editorial coverage. If you need coverage of your new product in particular magazines, you'd better be advertising in them. You also need to negotiate hard for preferred page positioning in each magazine.

To win in this critical buying process, you need to take advantage of every source of leverage you can muster. First of all, you have no choice but to hire one of the huge media-buying services. All of the major advertising agency networks have them. There are also a couple of independent ones. Buying services pool all their client's media dollars to maximize their clout with media vendors—that is, TV networks and magazine-publishing groups.

The major buying decision you must make each year is whether to participate in the TV up-front market, in which you commit to a lot of media over a twelve-month period, rather than going it quarter by quarter, making scatter buys. The advantages of going up front are that you get better programming and lock in guaranteed rates. The downside is that you reduce your financial flexibility somewhat, although this can be mitigated by partial cancellation rights and the ability to move spots within a broadcast quarter. Another potential drawback is that the scatter market may come in lower than upfront rates, although this has only happened twice in the past twenty years. Increasingly, magazine pages are also bought based on annual agreements, with similar trade-offs.

Needless to say, it takes a strong stomach to be a media buyer, particularly when it comes to up-front TV buying. Billions of dollars get committed in a totally unpredictable couple of weeks, days, or even hours. Many of the key buyer/seller relationships go back years and years. Make sure you have a direct relationship with your buyer and that he or she knows what you expect.

CMO Checkpoints

1. Media-buying is the single largest expense you will manage as a marketer. Give it the attention it deserves.
2. There's more than one way to plan a media budget. Combine all three methods—benchmarking, the task method, and the pragmatic method.
3. Let your knowledge of your target audience guide your selection of media channels.
4. Treat ratings points with a grain of salt—they're helpful but not gospel.
5. When scheduling ads, consider recency as well as frequency. Consumers have been proven to buy based on just one exposure to a good ad.
6. Curb costs by locking in rates, bundling buys, and demanding discounts.

Product Publicity

As the saying goes, an ounce of publicity is worth a pound of paid advertising. Especially for introductions, publicity can make or break your product or brand. To win at this critical part of the marketing mix, you need to understand how publicity works, what drives results, and how to get the most out of the publicity professionals on your team.

Media Mentions Matter

Product publicity—all those great editorial mentions of your brand in newspapers, in magazines, and on TV—sells product in two distinctly different ways. First, because publicity has much more source credibility than advertising, it acts as a third-party endorsement that at times can even rival the influence of the almighty word of mouth. Almost all media mentions are, in effect, endorsements that create a buzz around your brand. Despite the media literacy—and the media skepticism—of many consumers today, mentions in the media that come via editorial coverage rather than paid advertising can break through consumers' mental defenses and get under their radar. The first great strength of well-executed publicity is that consumers perceive it to be unbiased.

Another reason why product publicity is effective is simply that it is much less expensive per media impression delivered than paid advertising. In other words, you don't even need the implied editorial endorsement for publicity to work. Often, editorial mentions include disclaimers such as, "According to the manufacturer, Brand X does such and such." But even this relatively unbiased reporting is valuable—it gets your name and your claim announced. And delivery of a message is the first step toward brand awareness.

Key Drivers of Publicity: Newsworthiness and Entertainment Value

Newsworthiness is the original coin of the publicity realm. If something is newsworthy, it gets the attention of the editorial side of media companies. Editorial is the "product" that media companies sell to their readers, listeners, or viewers. If you can provide newsworthy information—

information that can be used to beef up their editorial, they will return the favor by mentioning your brand. Simple as that.

But what is newsworthy about a consumer brand? To begin with, it is the same thing that is advertising-worthy— that is, a message that is meaningfully different. Chances are, if you have a compelling brand positioning that is supported by a strongly performing product, you will be able to drive publicity, too. Crest White Strips, the first home-use product that really did whiten teeth, was inherently newsworthy. It got a lot of well-deserved publicity as a genuine product breakthrough. But often you can create "new news" for long-established products. The research showing that aspirin reduces the chance of heart attacks was big news when it came out, over a hundred years after the launch of the first aspirin.

Increasingly, as the Hollywoodization of our culture continues, publicity generation is also about entertainment. Our civilization is besotted by entertainment. There are now countless TV shows, radio programs, magazines, books, and websites dedicated specifically to delivering entertainment "news." Some of these entertainment news outlets consist of little more than a string of press releases. More significantly, even the so-called serious media is subtly being taken over by entertainment content and values. Nowadays, when you don't have any real news to convey, you can often generate publicity for your brand simply by providing the ancillary benefit of helping to entertain people.

My favorite example of entertainment-driven publicity was by Rold Gold pretzels. In an incredible stunt, Jason Alexander made a mock parachute jump into the stadium during the middle of the Super Bowl. There was no product news. There was no mega-brand budget. Just flawless conceptual and tactical craftsmanship. Al Michaels and the other game announcers acted their parts superbly. The postgame talk value and media coverage were huge. Rold Gold took full advantage of a live event while maintaining tight control (in contrast to the fruitless live Super Bowl taste test run by Schlitz several years before). The stunt was homage to Orson Wells's "War of the Worlds" radio broadcast, which convinced thousands of people that the Martians really had landed. It was wildly entertaining. And it sold a lot of pretzels.

Regardless of which type of publicity mentions you generate—news-generated buzz or entertainment-generated hype—make a mantra out of the phrase *media mentions matter*. More is more. Set goals for mentions. Measure your mentions. You can also translate your mentions into advertising currency by calculating how much paid media value your publicity-generated mentions equal. Keep in mind that a five-second editorial mention can be worth more than a thirty-second ad because of the implied endorsement. Many brands shoot to match the value of their publicity mentions to their entire media budgets. And again, the magic of publicity is that it costs only a fraction of the media value you get.

Setting the Stage for Great Publicity

Publicity efforts as great as Rold Gold's Super Bowl stunt don't just happen. You have to set the stage. Prepare for success by considering publicity during product design, building relationships with PR agencies, and working the media.

Design Publicity into Your Product

The time to start thinking about generating publicity on a new product or brand is at its inception. Just as you build advertisability into your brand during its design stage, publicity messages, too, start early.

Wine companies offer a good example of building in publicity at the outset, starting with the selection of where to source the grapes. Gallo gets most of its grapes from the vast Central Valley of California. When Gallo wanted to go upscale, its first move was to buy some prime real estate in the prestigious Sonoma Valley. During the several years that it took to plant vineyards and create an upscale wine, the publicity machine was running full tilt. Gallo also cleverly used Gina Gallo, a granddaughter of one of the founders, to differentiate the new, higher-end Gallo from the company's jug-wine mainstays. Gina's youth and new attitude toward wine making was the focus of all of the premium wine communication.

Leveraging Publicity Experts

Specialized communication firms known as public relations agencies handle most product publicity work. Many PR agencies handle additional tasks, including investor relations, crisis management, community affairs, and corporate publicity. Other agencies focus exclusively on what they sometimes call marketing public relations, that is, product publicity. Regardless of the type of firm you hire, keep in mind that PR is very much a relationship business. You are primarily buying access to a few dozen key editorial decision makers at most. One talented person may be all you need or can afford. Many of these people choose to work out of small boutiques that have very little overhead to cover.

One of the best ways to identify an appropriate PR firm for your business is to ask some of the editorial people you are trying to influence. If you don't yet know these people, ask for introductions through their advertising sales colleagues. Look for an agency that has established credentials but also one that will consider you relatively important. You may need to combine all or most of your brands in order to become a top-priority client. Also, look for an agency that works on highly complementary product categories. That client mix will tend to give the agency the most relevant expertise and contact base.

The best way to get good work from your PR agency is to let the agency team inside your strategic tent. This means habitually copying your PR people on key documents. It means regular face-to-face meetings. It means not overdelegating the responsibility for the relationship on your side. It means giving clear direction and listening hard to their recommendations. It means being the squeaky wheel. Try to get at least one big win per brand per year. Celebrate the accomplishments. And, very important, don't waste your PR agency's time on program pitches you are simply not open to. A quick no is far better than a slow one.

Working the Media

Having a publicity-friendly product and an appropriate, well-directed PR agency will take you a long way toward creating competitive advantage in your publicity efforts. It also helps if you design your overall work flow to be media friendly. To do so, keep the following in mind.

Timing Is Everything The cardinal sin in publicity is to go to the media too late, after the news horse has left the barn. If the consumer has already been exposed to your new product, there's just no reason for the media to cover it. As the chairman of Twentieth Century Fox told me upon my arrival in Hollywood, "The ice cube melts." Make sure your ice cubes are in good shape by getting in front of long-lead-time media outlets with the finished story well within their deadlines.

Fortunately, you and your PR agency don't need to have the final product before you meet with the media. Assuming your company has a solid reputation for doing what it says it will do, prototype versions can actually be a plus since media people think they are getting an inside scoop. As soon as you have the ideas together plus high-quality photography, you're ready to go. Of course, if you have the luxury of more finished samples or even line-produced product, you should use them. And if you have examples of the product's market impact, from either a test market or a launch in another country, use that as well.

Provide a Context Give the media some context to work with. Most product publicity is served with at least some general, non-brand-specific information. Many marketers commission special consumer surveys—well crafted to put their product in its best light, of course—that the media can position as real news to viewers or readers. It's a mistake to treat editors as mere shills for new products; they need to have a broad-based story in which to weave the new-product mention. Imagine a Venn diagram with one circle containing brand-specific information, most of which is relatively uninteresting to the general population, and the other circle containing interesting, though non-brand-specific information. The area where the two circles overlap is the publicity sweet spot. Finding and maximizing the sweet spot is the central challenge of product publicity.

You need to make sure that the bait you use to get the media's attention ultimately grows out of and leverages what Leo Burnett famously called the brand's "inherent drama." At the same time, you must give editors some broader information to weave it into. When Rogaine was launched, much of the publicity kit was about the psychological trauma of male-pattern baldness in general. When Jergens approached the media seeking publicity for its innovative shave-minimizing moisturizer, its PR team was armed with lots of interesting information on shaving and moisturizing in general.

Get Creative Be as creative with each news outlet as you try to be with each power retailer. Suggest several angles to work with. NBC is trying just as hard to differentiate itself from ABC as Target is from Wal-Mart or as you are from Brand X. In some cases, depending on how concentrated your news outlet industry is, you may want to consider offering exclusives, at least on certain aspects of the launch. But be careful, you don't want to alienate those who don't get the exclusive.

Listen and Learn Leverage the media for uses besides publicity. Like other suppliers, media contacts can bring fresh ideas into your organization. If you have the clout to get an audience with the producers of target broadcast shows or the publisher of key magazines, leverage it. Like your brand managers, these individuals are true monomaniacs with a mission who are often inspiring in their zeal for their product. They are informed by the massive amount of consumer feedback they get, especially with respect to magazine content. They are also a bit like bees that move from advertiser to advertiser, subtly if unintentionally cross-pollinating each along the way. You can't help but learn from them.

Types of Publicity Programs

There are almost as many types of product publicity as there are product categories. Figuring out what's appropriate for your particular situation depends on the newness, size, and nature of your brand. It also depends on the imagination of you and your publicity team.

The Press Kit

The most basic and most common publicity tool is the press kit. These typically consist of a carefully worded written summary—the press release—plus some product photography and some sort of hook to make your product news stand out in the slosh pit of other press kits. Your key job is to make sure the content of the press release is as powerful, accurate, and succinct as it possibly can be—especially the headline. Your PR agency should be able to counsel you on what hooks will stand out and what level of expense is appropriate, but you or someone on your staff also needs to be directly involved.

Publicity Stunts

Publicity stunts are the big enchiladas of the business. They are true productions, frequently costing hundreds of thou-

Editorial Hooks

Often, a good hook is nothing more than a small, brand-appropriate gift for the editors. Even a quality pen with your logo can do the trick. Other times, you need to escalate to a very fancy lunch—The Tavern on The Green in Central Park is a typical choice—a massage, a face-to-face meeting in the editor's office (known as a desk-side briefing), or a full-scale editor event, complete with presentations from you and from a well-known topic expert. Keep in mind that editors are very busy people and are inundated with invitations to product launches. Protect your reputation as someone who doesn't waste their time on small stuff, but call in your chips and demand their participation when you've got the goods.

One underutilized method of defraying costs and improving impact is to invite the financial analysts to your launch events as well as the media. Doing so may even help you land your CEO or at least your CFO. If so, make sure the editors know he or she is coming, and you will most likely get a better turnout than otherwise.

sands of dollars and requiring months of preparation from a large cast of experts. While common for blockbuster movies, publicity stunts are only cost-justifiable for the most major of new consumer product launches, such as Vanilla Coke or Windows 2000. Although stunts are usually staged

Hollywood: Publicity Central

Feature films are the most publicity-driven products. The release of a new movie is both news and entertainment, after all. The publicity value of each element is carefully considered and weighted heavily in each phase of development. Is the script from a hot writer? If not, is it at least from a well-known one? Is the subject topical? Can it attract A-level talent for both behind and in front of the camera? Will it fit into a publicity-friendly time slot, such as fall for highbrow films eligible for Oscar hype or summer for blockbuster popcorn movies? Is there a killer scene that can worm its way into news broadcasts? As you read through the following examples of exemplary film publicity, think about how you could adapt some of these ideas to your brand:

- *The scene in* Independence Day *where the aliens blew up the White House touched a collective nerve that mesmerized the media and moviegoers alike. It was the ultimate sight bite, perfect for signing off the evening news. A simple ploy like the movie's title—also its release date—built in extra publicity leverage, too.* Independence Day *even had a nickname, ID4. It owned July 4th. When I was working on the video release of this $300 million blockbuster, we eagerly leveraged such media-friendly snippets as Will Smith proclaiming,*

"I have got to get me one of these." In the film, he was referring to an alien ship he was driving. In our publicity, we had him use this line in reference to the videocassette of the movie. What's your brand's killer sight bite that can have a life of its own? Can you establish a time of year that you own?

- The Blair Witch Project *pulled off the incredible publicity stunt of convincing millions of moviegoers that it was actually a documentary of a lost group of teenagers. It employed shaky, handheld cameras and unknown actors in a tale of ultimate horror. The media played along as co-conspirators in the well-designed hoax, providing tens of millions of dollars of pseudo media coverage. The hoax was so complete, it retained a shroud of mystery even six months later, when the video was released. Can you think of any ways to add suspense to your brand or to give it some cultist cachet?*

- Titanic *is the biggest box office hit of all time. During its production stage, however, it was a nightmare for its primary bankroller, Twentieth Century Fox. The constant media reports of hundred-million-dollar cost overruns and shooting delays kept it in the limelight month after month. When the studio chairman went down to Mexico (where a huge replica of the Titanic had been built) to confront the film's director, James Cameron, that meeting even made the news. The entertainment media was on a feeding frenzy, and it didn't help that the*

(continued)

title of the movie has been synonymous with disaster for nearly a hundred years. Of course, when the film finally made it to the big screen, it had universal awareness, in this case proving that any publicity is good publicity, even when it's bad.

live in front of thousands of consumers, their actual target audience is the millions of prospects that the media relays the event to. The live audience serves largely as a prop.

Sometimes it's possible to stage low-cost but well-covered events even for a relatively small product. For the launch of the first "Simpsons" computer game, we found a suburb of Las Vegas called, you guessed it, Springfield. To generate publicity, we painted a house to look just like the colorful TV house and then ran a contest to give it away. The media couldn't resist the layers of sheer weirdness. (Las Vegas is weird. A town in the desert named Springfield is weird. A house painted to look like a cartoon is weird.) The success of the product behind the publicity helped establish Fox as a bona fide supplier of computer and video games.

The key is having an unusual degree of distinctiveness in the product, the programs, or preferably, both.

The Annual Equity Event

Some of the most powerful consumer product publicity has nothing to do with new products. I'm referring to events that are repeated year after year—the annual equity event. The media coverage of who makes it onto the Wheaties box is huge. Congratulations to General Mills on this one. The Super Bowl "I'm going to Disney World" program is another great evergreen event. In both these cases, the execution just gets better each year through sheer practice.

The Meow Mix cat food Meow Off was a classic in the genre of annual events. The name of the event made it brand specific. The basic content of the event, cats auditioning to be in a Meow Mix commercial (using the highly newsworthy "Meow, meow, meow, cats ask for it by name" campaign), was inherently interesting. Plus, the event lent itself to the format of a grassroots contest moving from local to regional to national. The Meow Off ran for several years and helped build the brand to the second-place share position in its market. Several soap companies have attempted to run similar events centering on singing in the shower, but they have lacked the brand specificity and the inherent appeal of the Meow Off.

Packaging- and Product-Based Publicity

The Apple iMac's launch was all about its cool graphics. A long time ago, Braniff Airlines got massive publicity from painting its aircraft in wild colors. In 2002 Tide commissioned a famous clothing designer to create Warholesque Tide-wear—and got mentions. Gogurt, a huge success, is just yogurt in a squeeze tube. The updates of Betty Crocker and Aunt Jemima get a lot of ink. But you can leverage more than just what's new in packaging.

Sometimes all you need to do to get the media's attention is to bring back old packaging, especially if you are working on a really old brand. Ivory soap did this in 2001. Maxwell House coffee did it several years before. Quaker Oats has brought back old versions of the Quaker man. Life cereal has brought back Mikey (of "Even Mikey likes it" fame) several times.

On the product front, M&M and Life Saver candy have both generated lots of publicity by running contests to pick their new color and flavor, respectively. Ben & Jerry's has run similar programs to name new ice-cream flavors.

Trickle-Down Publicity

Sometimes, product publicity uses the medium of influential consumers rather than magazines, newspapers, TV, or radio. The idea is to enlist heavy users or the category tastemakers in a word-of-mouth campaign. Music companies often target college radio stations, knowing that popular DJs can have an influence far beyond their direct listeners. The makers of Botox, the recently approved antiwrinkle drug, sponsored a series of Botox Parties, which quickly spread the word that a dramatic new option was available in the fight against time. The key to the success of this program was its selection of influential hosts for the parties.

Cause-Related Publicity

Revlon has sponsored a number of fund-raising events that have helped position that company and brand as a solid citizen in the fight against breast cancer. Paul Mitchell hair care publicizes that it is against animal testing. Paul Newman salad dressing makes a charitable donation for each bottle sold. And, of course, the Body Shop created its entire market positioning via publicity about its efforts to foster sustainable development among rain forest tribes and other threatened indigenous peoples.

Advertising as Publicity

Sometimes just having an incredible ad is enough to get the publicity machine going. Ads with this kind of power are few and far between and sometimes don't sell product, but when they work, it's an amazing sight to behold. Apple Computer's "1984" spot for its Macintosh PC is a classic example. Budweiser has gotten good publicity mileage out of its frog ads and repeated its success with its "Wasssssuuupppp?" campaign. Nike has had a number of contenders, including the 2002 retro NBA ad. Alka Seltzer had a couple of standouts ("I can't believe I ate the whole thing"; "That's a spicy meatball"). Coke had its "Teach the world to sing" campaign, the music from which was turned into a popular song, gaining regular radio play. Coke also had "Mean Joe Green." Pepsi advertising is most famous for Michael Jackson's burning-hair accident. Taco Bell had the talking chihuahua. Parkay margarine had "Butter." Absolut vodka ads become famous as works of art. And, of course, there is Wendy's "Where's the beef?"—a line that made it into the presidential debates.

Product Placement

Product placement in movies and TV shows is a specialty arm of product publicity. We all know what Will Smith and Tommy Lee Jones did for Ray Ban sunglasses in the two *Men in Black* movies. Product placement burst onto the consumer product radar screen when Reese's Pieces leveraged a cameo appearance in *E.T., the Extraterrestrial* to significantly grow its distribution and sales. My advice is not to hire a product placement firm but to be ready to generously provide samples to any TV show or film producer who asks. If you have a unique or widely known brand, you will get placement regardless of your or your agency's efforts. And samples are cheap.

Like other aspects of publicity, having something that is visually differentiated helps a lot. When Alberto VO5 was quite prominently placed behind Al Pacino in a key locker room scene in *Any Given Sunday*, we didn't notice a sales blip. On the other hand, when Mel Gibson used a Bioré Pore Strip in *What Women Want*, the brand had a significant sales uptick. It also helped that Bioré had a 70 percent share of the pore-strip market.

Advertorials

Don't overlook the space that exists between normal paid advertising and publicity-generated editorial coverage, that is, the advertorial. Many teen magazines, for example, will write up and produce a several-pages-long themed advertorial featuring your product in a style fairly similar to their normal editorial style. The price is often no more than the price of a single ad, plus the cost of production. You can negotiate the right to see the layouts and copy before the advertorial goes to press.

Be careful about TV advertorials (sponsored productions), however. The producers of these are seldom willing or able to give you a chance to review the film prior to airing. Also, they often cannot guarantee the segment you are financially subsidizing will even make it on air.

CMO Checkpoints

1. Publicity has two key strengths. It can deliver both more credibility and more cost-effectiveness than paid advertising. Media mentions matter!
2. Newsworthiness and entertainment value are the key drivers of publicity.
3. Build publicity into your new products from the outset.
4. Timing is everything. Make sure the media sees your news long before your consumers do.
5. Make a point of spending time with key publishers and editors for your industry. They are full of new-product ideas and consumer insights.
6. The major thing PR agencies provide is relationships you can leverage with key media people. Make sure your agency really has these.
7. Study the entire business universe for publicity approaches that could work for your brand. Search and reapply.

Retailers

Retailers are your direct customers. As a marketer, you need *customer* insights almost as much as you need *consumer* insights. And just like consumers, retailers are evolving rapidly. To stay ahead with consumers, you need to stay ahead with your retail customers.

Changes in Retailing

Many changes have transformed the landscape of consumer marketing over the past few years but none so significantly as the rise of what are commonly referred to as power retailers. Not since the invention of television has anything stirred up the marketing environment as much as the advent of power retailing. As marketers, our jobs have quickly evolved. We used to market to consumers through a large number of relatively homogeneous, somewhat passive retailers. Now we comarket to consumers in partnership with a handful of very heterogeneous, very proactive retailers.

The causes of this revolution go beyond channel blurring and massive retailer consolidation, although these are big factors. Retailers have simply gotten a lot smarter. Of course, they have the scanner data that helps them know their business better than ever. And, yes, they have satellite-connected distribution systems. But the biggest change is that they have learned from their suppliers how to be brand marketers. The leading mass-channel retailers, Wal-Mart, Target, Kmart, Kroger, Albertson's, Ahold, Safeway, HEB, Walgreens, CVS, Rite Aid, Eckerd's, Dollar General, and Costco, all have differentiated brand positionings, integrated marketing communications, and robust store-label programs. They also have a raft of their own marketing programs, for which they sell participations to their top suppliers. Moreover, power retailers have invested in buying and merchandising systems and in highly talented people to run them.

This is forcing manufacturers of consumer goods to respond in kind. It's no longer a euphemism to call a retail buyer a category manager. He or she really is. In job description and in practice, retailer category managers are as intensely focused on building market share and profit (in addition to good old volume) for their retail brand as the most sophisticated consumer brand marketers.

Power retailers have the potential to know their consumers better than consumer manufacturers ever could.

Some are starting to realize this potential. Frequent-shopper programs have been around for decades. Most people over forty can remember some form of stamps, particularly S&H Green Stamps, which rewarded store loyalty. Consumer manufacturers have tried many such programs themselves. Betty Crocker points on most General Mills products are a good example. Cigarette brands and Bazooka gum, too, have used the same strategy. But none of these loyalty programs come close to matching the sophistication of the scanner-based frequent-shopper programs most grocery chains now use. Making massive amounts of behavioral (versus self-reported) data available for the first time, these programs take power retailers way beyond simple price promotion to something approaching real relationship marketing.

Today's power retailers are truly the buying agents for the consumers of the world. Not only do they "Give the lady what she wants," but they do so at remarkably competitive prices. The wastefulness that once led to high prices has been eliminated by power retailers, as has much of the high-low pricing, the practice of drawing in customers with steep sales cuts one week, only to ratchet up prices again the next. In its place, everyday low pricing (EDLP) is the stated goal, if not the full daily practice of most power retailers. EDLP reduces total system costs for manufacturers and retailers, and the fierce competition that results ensures that these savings are passed on to consumers.

The overall efficiency and consumer focus of power retailers put considerable pressure on manufacturers to sharpen their demand creation skills, especially regarding consumer insights, technical innovation, and advertising (creative quality and media levels). Even a few years ago, manufacturers could buy their way on to store shelves through exorbitant trade deals, slotting allowances, or buyer hospitality. That's just not the case now. The irony of all this is that the rise of the power retailers has helped put the consumer marketers' focus more than ever on the consumer. The way to win with power retailers is to win with consumers. In other words, the way to win is to create power brands, the topic of every chapter in this book.

It's a Wal, Wal, Wal, Wal-Mart World

For most consumer product companies, Wal-Mart is not only their top customer by a factor of three or four but also their fastest-growing one—and has been for ten years running with no end in sight! This does not even factor in Wal-Mart's wholesale division, Sam's Club. To top it off, Wal-Mart doesn't even demand slotting allowances, a topic covered later in this chapter. Wal-Mart is already the world's largest company, bigger than General Motors and bigger than Exxon-Mobil. It will almost certainly be the world's first trillion-dollar business.

In spite of all the stories of Wal-Mart destroying the downtown shopping districts of hundreds of towns, there has never been a more benign colossus. Wal-Mart plays fair. If you're a small supplier, this is one retailer who will always give you the benefit of the doubt. They are an open-book

test. You know in advance that to pass to the next grade—
that is, to make it through the next shelf-set review (known
as the *modular review* in Wal-Mart-speak or *planogram* at
other retailers)—each of your products must sell a known
number of pieces per store per week.

Wal-Mart is also squeaky clean. For instance, buyers are
not allowed to accept any gifts. Wal-Mart rotates buyers
often, partly to learn more businesses but largely to ensure
they don't get cozy with sellers. And until they just got too
big for it to make sense, Wal-Mart discouraged manufacturers from locating sales reps at its Arkansas headquarters,
to avoid out-of-office relationships. The company didn't
want to make it hard for a buyer to say no to his or her
child's Little League coach. Wal-Mart's drive to avoid even
the appearance of impropriety has made the entire consumer universe among the most ethical business sectors
anywhere. With a relentless focus on what truly adds value
to its 100 million weekly shoppers, Wal-Mart has done
more than any company to stomp out the waste that was
once rampant in consumer marketing.

Wal-Mart's core competitive weapon remains, of
course, its talented, well-managed, million-strong work-
force. Thanks to a rewarding stock-option program, even
in a company with hundreds of billions in sales, the person on the sales floor acts like an owner. Combining this
strength with its legendary information technology prowess
has made Wal-Mart almost unstoppable. Wal-Mart's geographical expansion strategy also should be credited for its
meteoric ascent. Wal-Mart has played the map like a mas-

ter of the board game Risk. Rather than make a premature grab for Kamchatka, Wal-Mart fights on one front at a time, dominating one region before moving on to the next. The company started in small-town Middle America and gradually expanded region by region and then to the bigger cities. Only after the U.S. market was wrapped up did Wal-Mart venture into international markets in a big way. First the retailer rolled up the rest of North America, aided by the acquisition of Woolworth's business in Canada and a joint venture with a leading Mexican chain. Wal-Mart stumbled a little in Germany but has since come on strong in Europe with the purchase of ASDA in the United Kingdom. The company's recent purchase of a stake in Japan's Seiyu chain has been greeted like an invasion from Walzilla by that country's highly fragmented retail community.

Wal-Mart has weaknesses, of course. Its TV advertising is less than exemplary, especially when compared to Target's. The ghost of the legendary Sam Walton is inevitably starting to fade from the company's culture. Costco continues to outperform Sam's Club in the wholesale-club market. Executives are still ticked off at themselves about "that quarter," the one that was supposed to set a record for 100 quarters of consecutive profit growth.

Make no mistake, though. Wal-Mart is the one retailer to which all consumer marketers need to tailor their value chain. Increasingly, this means locating more and more personnel at Wal-Mart headquarters in Arkansas. It means making investments in customer service that approach six-sigma quality, including inventory management. It means never introducing a new product without consulting with Wal-Mart buyers, at least regarding timing. It means never taking a price increase without a special justification meeting and memo. Overall, it means giving Wal-Mart an extraordinary level of top-management time and attention.

Retail Objectives

Retailers are powerful partners in delivering brand value to consumers. They are also your fierce competitors in capturing the profits that come from doing so. You need more than power brands to get your "fair share" of the profits. You also need smart promotion plans and sharp negotiation skills. First, though, you have to be clear about what you want. Fortunately, although retail practices have changed quite drastically in recent decades, marketers' fundamental objectives—distribution, pricing, shelf placement, and merchandising—have not.

Distribution

Nothing can happen until you get the product not only authorized at headquarters for distribution but actually cut in at the individual store level. When your salespeople tell you they got distribution of a new item, be sure to ask whether it replaced another one of your products—a tradeout—or they got incremental distribution. Also ask whether the product is in all stores in the chain or just in the bigger shelf-sets. Better yet, make sure you get out into the field and help your sales force do the selling.

The way to get new products into distribution is to have propositions that have a good shot at building sales and profits for the category—not just your own brand. In other words, you need a consumer-attracting idea that is well executed and supported by enough marketing investment to be heard above the clutter. And don't forget the simple necessity of getting your story and sales samples to customers on time. Power retailers have set times when they review categories for distribution changes. Work with their timing. Finally, don't neglect trying to get old products into new distribution, too.

Pricing

You need to push hard to get your everyday shelf prices as low as possible, recognizing retailers naturally take higher margins on new or small brands or products. If your brand is in a large category in which consumers comparison shop and if you have achieved leadership or are near it, push for leadership retailer margins (low ones). Although retailer category managers and buyers hate to do this, since it hurts their individual profit scorecard, it is often in the retailer's overall best interest. It is a good way to make a statement in their market and thus draw traffic to their stores. Again, be vigilant that you are competitively priced in all stores, not just the big sets.

Shelf Placement

As in real estate, when it comes to retail distribution, the key is location, location, location. Eye level is the preferred vertical spot for almost every brand, but not always. The velocity of Suave shampoo is so high that Helene Curtis used to request the bottom shelf for it. The bottom shelf often holds more bottles than the smaller eye-level shelves, so that placement reduced out-of-stocks. The best horizontal spot for a brand is next to the category or segment leader or toward the end of the aisle, where consumers first enter the category.

But sometimes the decision is quite tricky. Olay decided to push for retail placement of its new hand and body lotion in the facial care section, since it was high priced and the brand—and company—had no established home in the hand and body lotion section. And sometimes a brand is powerful enough to get that great perk of success, dual distribution. Jergens Naturally Smooth, the first shave-minimizing moisturizer, was innovative enough that several retailers shelved it in both the lotion set and the shaving set. Chances are, you have some shelving opportunity you haven't yet exploited. Keep in mind that power retailers are quite willing to do a shelving test if you present solid rationale to do so.

Merchandising

Focus your attention on getting into the key events of the power retailers. Long gone are the days when manufacturers had the clout to get retailers to tie in to the manufacturer's events (other than a very few special circumstances). Make sure you know when they are making decisions and what their brand selection criteria are. Find out what their overall merchandizing objectives are, and go to them proactively with ways your brands can help them meet their goals. Making accurate financial evaluations of proposed programs often requires the participation not only of sales and marketing but also of finance and operations. This is particularly true when it involves the need for capital expenditures, such as when a special size is requested. Recognize that many programs that retailers encourage you to participate in simply don't pay out. You need to win the war in the store, but you also need money for other things such as advertising and profit.

Optimizing Total Trade Spending

Total trade promotion expenses represent anywhere from 5 to 30 percent of the consumer manufacturer's sales dollar. The average is 15 percent of gross sales, making trade promotion one of the biggest single expense items in the marketing budget. Even the most powerful brands require some level of trade promotion as incentives for retailers to support them. And today the definition of trade spending has expanded to include many new elements that need to be mastered.

How Trade Promotion Has Evolved

One of the best ways to maximize the return on your trade promotion investment is to understand how it has evolved over time. This will give you a sense of where trade promotion is heading. Twenty years ago, a typical postintroductory trade allowance was offered by brand manufacturers two or three times a year and nominally lasted three to four weeks per deal. Often, the deal was broken into x percent for a display, y percent for a feature ad, and z percent for a price reduction. A key metric back then was percent on deal. The toughest retailers negotiated early buys, forward buys, and late buys so that they would never have to pay the regular price. Some of them built huge warehouses for the extra inventory and went into the diverter business. Diverters became expert at buying on the deepest deal (typically at the end of a manufacturer's fiscal year or half) and then reselling the goods to other retailers. Gradually the percents on deal climbed, until in the early 1990s they were so high that they made a mockery of the entire system. Back then, manufacturers also had wordy promotional contracts that required retailer "performance" in order to collect allowances. The cheapest way to perform was to run an ad, so retailers ran ads, lots of them. For several years, the ads got so small they were referred to as obituary ads or revenue ads. Retail buyers were making merchandising decisions based on collecting allowances, almost irrespective of whether or not their actions stimulated consumer demand.

Eventually, the whole system mutated from one-off allowances to annual accrual funds. Accrual funds were originally based on x percent of the prior year's sales. The beauty of the system at first was that the total funds available were known up front, theoretically allowing the retail buyer and manufacturer's sales rep to "sit down and plan the year" with an eye on the consumer. Quickly, however, the problem of dealing with the great variations among retailers' growth rates changed this. The idea of "live funds" was invented to ensure that fast-growing retailers got more funding than slower-growing or shrinking retailers. This just turned the game back to the old approach of using trade allowance percents. But, importantly, the focus on a joint six- to twelve-month planning period remained intact.

Retailers' move to EDLP (everyday low pricing), initiated by Wal-Mart, Dollar General, and others, forced other changes in trade promotion practices. These power retailers demanded and to a large extent got the dead, dead, dead net price—in other words, the price after all off-invoice allowances, accruals, bill-backs, and other discounts had been applied. Their broad argument was that their best merchandising vehicle was not a feature ad or even a short-term end-cap display, but rather a reduced price at shelf every single day. As a result, many consumer product companies reduced their reported net sales because the price allowances effectively became permanent price reductions. In 2002, reporting net sales at the lower level became a financial standard.

From Trade Promotion to Customer Profitability

The rise of the power retailer has led to the rise of the power sales force. Salespeople—or customer business managers (CBMs), as they are now usually called—have made a parallel leap in skill sets, resources, and raw power within their own companies. Relationships with buyers still count for a lot, as does product knowledge and general selling acumen. But increasingly, salespeople earn their stripes by penetrating not just the customer but also their own company's decision-making process. As the voice of the customer, they have a major say in priorities, new products, staffing, timing, and anything else that affects the company's go-to-market strategy. The bottom line for CBMs is not sales volume, it's predictable, capital-efficient, profitable volume. This focus on customer-by-customer profitability is very similar to the focus on brand-by-brand profit in the marketing function.

CBMs still spend a lot of time managing trade promotion spending. There is immense pressure to invest each dollar productively. It's not easy. Doing well takes a close working relationship with many functions, especially marketing. The return on investment (ROI) analyses done on slotting allowances, for example, are every bit as thorough as those done for a new-product launch. Become joined at the hip with your sales team. Become as familiar with their customers' scorecards—that is, the measures retailers use to measure vendor performance—as you can. Remember, every successful brand is not just marketing driven, it's sales driven, too.

Returns, Markdowns, and Closeouts

When new products fail or when products get damaged or spoiled, everyone in the business chain just wishes they would disappear. Unfortunately, that isn't what happens. As a marketer, you can have a big impact here by bending over backward to avoid launching ill-conceived or poorly executed new products that end up stapled to the shelf. You can also help by working with your packaging department to come up with durable packaging on all your products. It may help to take an engineer or two to one of your customer's distribution centers. Let the engineers see how much physical violence is inflicted on a package when shipping cases are torn open and individual pieces are heaved into the totes that many retailers, especially drug chains, use to ship product out to their stores. It's a scene reminiscent of the old Samsonite luggage gorilla ads.

You can also work closely with your sales force to put in place coherent long-term policies for dealing with the inevitable problems that arise. Policies are a lot more efficient than requiring that the whole team get together to debate each occurrence. In doing this, keep in mind that a markdown allowance, which shows up as a trade deal on your P&L statement, may very well be better from a total systems perspective than waiting for a return. Returns, though costly, somehow disappear from your financials because they get recorded as simply a sale that never happened. Some retailers have pushed for and some manufacturers have accepted trading terms that call for applying a standard allowance to cover mishaps in all cases. If you have enough stability in your back data, you should consider terms like this as a way to reduce administrative costs on both sides.

Payment Terms

No company wants to be the banker for its trading partners by supplying interest-free credit. Still, the reality is that your invoices are not going to be paid as soon as you would like. Big, powerful companies like Procter & Gamble insist on payment within twenty days, but most manufacturers offer retailers thirty days to pay up. Often, the wait stretches into forty days. Smaller companies even offer extended dating as another incentive to get retailers to take on new products. Be on the lookout for requests for consignment selling. Selling on consignment means you won't get paid by the retailer until the product has been sold to—and paid for by—the end user. Consignment selling is a CFO's nightmare; avoid it at all costs.

Service-Based Pricing

Service-based pricing means charging your retail customers different prices for the same physical product, with the differences depending on how many ancillary services you bundle with it. This makes pricing much more complicated than it has been in the past. How do you charge customers for retail sales coverage? For inventory planning? For special shipping configurations? Before you move too aggressively into customization, make sure you have thought through the complexities and have a first-class cost-accounting team at the ready.

Quantity Discounts

Most manufacturers have set up several pricing brackets that depend on whether the customer orders a full truckload, half load, or some fraction of a load. The pressure to reduce inventories while increasing service creates a lot of tension here. Make sure your logistics team understands the total system costs of the various options.

Payment Deductions

Sometimes retailers unilaterally decide not to pay. Perhaps this is for good reason—such as a short shipment on your part, for example. At other times, payment reductions are due to simple clerical errors. Sometimes, though, retailers make payment deductions just because they can or fiscally must. The simpler you can keep your dealing with trade partners, the fewer deductions you will have to work through.

Trade Advertising

Bah humbug to placing ads in trade magazines! The only thing these ads are good for is giving away secrets to your competitors. They are a horribly inefficient way to communicate with your retailers' decision makers. There are a few dozen retailers and maybe twice that number of individuals at those retailers who control the overwhelming majority of the shelf space and merchandising decisions for your categories. Your organization had better have close, direct, personal relationships established with all of them. That's why your company pays about 5 percent of every sales dollar to have a sales department and/or broker network.

Retailer Hospitality

Retailer entertainment, or hospitality, is another area of trade spending you can likely cut back on. Ten years ago,

Helene Curtis spent a lot of money taking customers to Hawaii. Clairol was famous for spending huge dollars taking buyers to the U.S. Tennis Open. But the economics of this kind of hospitality just stopped making sense. Some business sectors, especially those with many independent dealers to influence, can still get some benefit out of trade entertainment. Few beer distributors miss a Super Bowl, for example. But for most consumer product companies, major entertainment is a thing of the past.

Again, as in so many other areas, the impact of Wal-Mart and a few other key power retailers has been decisive. Wal-Mart simply won't allow their buyers to be entertained. Even when I was in Hollywood marketing packaged entertainment (home videos and computer games) and Wal-Mart and other big customers came to us (since all the studios are in the same place), senior managers of Wal-Mart would

Trade Advertising Waste

The consumer product industry is relatively immune to the trade advertising humbug. Real state-of-the-art foolishness is in the entertainment industry, which has not one but two daily trade rags. These are filled with underling-placed ads, congratulating bosses for being so wonderful. Their boss's boss should fire them for such waste, but, then, they are doing the same thing.

insist on paying for their own dinners. They did this to avoid even the appearance of impropriety. God bless the incorruptible.

Consumer Promotion

Since the rise of power retailers, most consumer promotion—other than product sampling—is better thought of as part of customer merchandising and trade promotion. The simple test for assigning a promotion's classification between consumer and customer is whether or not it's customer specific. Freestanding inserts (FSIs), the ubiquitous coupon "magazines" that come in Sunday newspapers, have some real advertising value and are genuine consumer trial events for new products. But as described below, FSIs are largely customer-specific trade events. Special packs, bonus packs, displayable pallets, and prepack displays are all very customer specific. They are also expensive, especially when you factor in the soft costs of creating, modifying, and reworking them.

Determining the return on investment for each piece of the marketing mix is harder than anyone would like. Promotional return is particularly problematic. This is especially true when it's planned and budgeted for by one group (marketing) but executed by another (sales). For decades, creative sales professionals have found ways to conserve on "their" money by dipping into headquarters' national consumer promotion money, with no incentive to care about effectiveness or efficiency. With the systems that have been in place, who can blame them?

The concept of customer profitability is a big step forward. More and more, the sales function is responsible for the planning, budgeting, and execution of all promotions that are customer specific, not just allowances and market development funds. Marketing's role is reduced to negotiating the total annual customer-directed budget percentage and to setting brand-equity-related guidelines such as the percent of special packs allowed for a given customer in a year. As you'd expect, once salespeople are made accountable for all the money they are spending, they take a much harder look at how all the dollars are spent. Handing off much of this work also enables marketers to do a better job at leading brand innovation, creating better national programs, and developing stronger advertising.

Coupons

FSI coupons are the smack of consumer marketing. We all know they're bad for us, but most of us just can't stop using them. Tune in, turn on, and drop some coupons. We'll still respect you on Sunday morning.

The great thing about coupons is that their ineffectiveness can be accurately measured. They never pay out. When you factor in the cost to distribute them (the media cost), the clearinghouse fees, the misredemptions, the subsidization of people who would have bought your brand anyway, as well as the face value of the coupon itself; you'd often be better off just taping dollar bills to each case you ship.

For these and other reasons, P&G ran a hugely publicized cold-turkey no-coupon test market in the Northeast a couple of years ago. And the truly coupon-addicted cereal companies are forever trying to go on coupon diets. Needless to say, however, the smack is back, although at a slightly lower purity level than a while back.

The rationale for coupons in recent years has been that they drive off-shelf merchandising, particularly the almighty end-cap display. The logic here is that you don't even want any redemptions, you just want the displays that the coupon drop supposedly forces the retailer to put up. Coupons were also rationalized because they forced distribution on new items. This still works to a certain extent for small (primarily grocery) retailers that can't afford to create their own merchandising plan. But it no longer works with the power retailers that account for the overwhelming majority of consumer sales. Their goal is to differentiate themselves from other retailers. They have their own programs that they expect suppliers to procure from them. They have little reason to tie in with a manufacturer's coupons that their retail competitors can just as easily accept. And be aware that mass merchandisers and drugstores have a particular aversion to FSIs. They know that FSIs, in effect, subsidize grocery chains at their expense. This is because consumers go to grocery stores more often and thus use more coupons there.

Enormous energy is expended on FSIs by promotion departments and the junior ranks of consumer marketing organizations. They battle it out for prime drop dates with the two FSI suppliers (News America and Valassis), which offer a decent semblance of category exclusivity. The big consumer companies have staked out annual tent-pole dates that they consistently anniversary. Gillette owns the World Series timing. P&G owns the key white-sale week (the first Sunday in January) with its Publisher's Clearing House event. Unilever has long dropped two times in July and refers to this as Suave Month. Things get particularly nasty with holiday or seasonal businesses such as candy and hand lotion. If you don't have an established tent pole, at least fight for the first Sunday in a month (to leverage social security checks and business pay weeks). Most importantly, try to focus your coupon investment on new products that stand to benefit the most from FSIs' power to create consumer awareness.

One of the long-standing justifications for coupons is the supposition that at least the value gets passed on to the consumer. In other words, at least there is a modicum of manufacturer control. This presumed pass-through efficiency is favorably compared to the historically low-pass-through rates of trade allowances. Here again, the power retailers have moved the cheese. When a Wal-Mart or a Target says it will reduce your brand's shelf price, the retailer actually does it. Many retailers will even let you pay only for product that is scanned at the lower price (although they still charge a premium price for this). These so-called scan-downs are a growing trend worldwide and have become the primary way to do price promotion in the United Kingdom.

Coupon misredemption is a huge tax on the consumer world that hurts all of the legitimate players. Several years ago, an FSI coupon was dropped for a nonexistent product, and it redeemed at near the category average! The culprits aren't just the hard-core gang-clipping, organized criminals but the proverbial white-haired coupon-clipping church and school clubs as well. In addition, how many of you have ever had a retail checkout clerk accept a coupon from you on the wrong size, variant, or even brand of product you were buying? And wouldn't it be great if video store clerks were as cavalier about return dates as grocery clerks are on coupon expiration dates?

Industry and company gumshoes are constantly fighting this misredemption virus. Lots of people are arrested every year. Technology is helping somewhat, especially the practice of bar-coding coupons. All of the coupon clearinghouses have been moved to Mexico, where the companies can afford to invest more person-hours in detailed checking. But never forget you are printing money every time you run a coupon. Caveat marketer.

Special Packs

The other major consumer promotion still in use today is special packs. Most special packs offer free bonus ounces of either the same product or a complementary item. Power retailers love 'em. Unlike coupons or rebates, they require no consumer preparation or follow-up. They're instant grat-ification. For the manufacturer/marketer, they are the surest way to grow a brand.

Special packs are also very challenging to manage effec-tively. If you do too many of them, you will cheapen your brand in the eyes of consumers. Picking the appropriate quantity is tricky. It's hard to track competition in this area, since many brands use the same UPCs for special packs and regular open stock. And the quantity doesn't tell the whole story. It's better to sell, say, fifteen weeks of normal busi-ness to Customer A and let the customer blow through it all in an end-cap promotion over two weeks than it is to sell, say, six weeks of normal volume to Customer B, who lets it sit on the regular shelf week after week.

Another problem with special packs is that they have a lot of costs, including ones that don't often show up in a brand's profit and loss statement. A special size may require a capital investment in new molds. Your manufacturing group will need to carry duplicate inventories, since not all customers take special packs. Some companies actually cre-ate triplicate inventory—they create special packs with and without different UPCs. Needless to say, special packs make it difficult to forecast sales accurately at the level where it counts—the individual SKU.

Again, the move to customer profitability should help you here. Leading companies now charge their salespeople for special packs (i.e. they take the money out of their trade funds), regardless of whether customers end up taking what they requested. This creates a powerful incentive to keep the communications flowing. Salespeople are also charged for the extra cost of putting products in prepacked displays. Customer profitability isn't a silver bullet, but it certainly rationalizes a complex process.

Sampling: The Last True Consumer Promotion

When you have a product with a detectable point of difference, even if it's only a sensory cue, sampling is often a great way to get initial trial. This is especially true in cases where one or two uses are all that's required for consumers to notice the difference. Although you should do sampling strictly for the consumer pull, you should make your retail partners fully aware of what you are doing. Even if they won't tie in with the sample drop, they will be impressed by your confidence in the product.

I had the joy of experiencing a sampling breakthrough back when I was the first brand manager on Finesse hair care. Finesse was the first "volatile silicone" conditioner. It had real performance superiority against every brand on the market; including a near three-to-one win over Flex, then the market leader. Just as importantly, it had a killer fragrance. Despite spotty distribution and suspect advertising creative, Finesse became the number one conditioner within two months of its sample drop. And who didn't get an Equal gumball? More recently, Listerine has used massive sampling, including broad-scale in-store events, to help create a runaway hit with its PocketPacks.

The real action these days is in highly targeted sampling. Given the exploding costs of mail or physical sampling, this is inevitable. The problem is that most consumer goods need to be targeted relatively broadly in order to meet shelf velocity minimums. The way most marketers square the circle is to sample only their heaviest user profile (not their actual heavy users but people who resemble their current heavy users in behavior or, at least, attitudes). Another frequently used tool is targeted co-op sampling, such as the gift boxes college kids get when they check into their dorms as freshmen. Quite recently, an ingenious method has been invented for sampling to people who read the magazines you typically advertise in. If you carefully stay below the postal weight requirements and refer to the sampled product as technically just a quality rendition of the real thing, the economics now work well for targeted in-magazine sampling.

The most common way to measure the effectiveness of sampling is through follow-up phone surveys. By comparing results from a representative group of sample recipients with a similar group of nonrecipients, you can see what percentage converted from the sample to a full-size purchase. Unfortunately, you'll likely end up with a number such as 14 percent that has no good outside empirical benchmarks you can compare to. Fortunately, over time, you can build your own internal benchmarks.

The jury is still out on Internet-based request sampling. Physique, P&G's failed "first new-to-the-world hair-care brand in twenty years," tried the technique. Although the Internet may greatly reduce the cost of getting the request, you still need to rely on the good old post office for fulfillment.

To summarize, retailers play a huge role in the marketing of consumer products today. They are both your partners in building your brands and your competitors in capturing profits that come from this. Work closely with your sales force to create programs that address retailers' varying needs. At the same time, never let an emphasis on the customer get in the way of your primary focus—the consumer.

CMO Checkpoints

1. Recognize that power retailers are the biggest thing to hit consumer marketing since TV.
2. Power retailers expect insights, innovation, and demand creation from their suppliers.
3. Be ready for the next generation of trade terms. New retailer demands are coming.
4. Give your sales force primary responsibility for all customer-specific promotion, which is basically everything except sampling.
5. Don't waste money on trade advertising or customer entertainment.
6. Cut back on coupons, or at least test a cutback.
7. When your product warrants it, lean into sampling.

New Products

The first imperative of every organization is growth. And the number one source of growth is new products—be they restages of existing products, line extensions of existing brands, or entirely new-to-the-world brands. This is why it is often said that new products are the lifeblood of the company. They can and should be its lifeblood, but if they're not managed well, they can turn out to be a bloodbath instead. While advertising is still job number one in consumer marketing, creating successful new products is a close second.

Types of New Products

From a marketing standpoint, a new product can be a brand that you restage as "new and improved." New products also include line extensions and, of course, entirely new brands. The marketing decisions vary somewhat depending on the kind of new product you are launching.

Restages

A company's new-product strategy is a core part of its overall corporate strategy—in fact, new products often dominate it. This dominance creates the first strategic issue with new products: sometimes growth opportunities for existing products are neglected as attention focuses on the newcomers. It's therefore important to start by remembering the importance of existing brands.

Very few existing brands are ever fully established. In fact, most remain completely unknown to many, many potential consumers. In other words, the brands have been undermarketed. If your predecessors have done their job and introduced a brand with an economically viable reason for being, your first job is to nurture and grow it. This requires going back to the fundamentals: awareness, trial, distribution, shelving, pricing, and merchandising.

The primary way to transform a small, existing brand into a large, established one is to put together a fully integrated marketing campaign, often called a *brand restage*. It is critical that you assemble and orchestrate a many-layered bundle of simultaneous initiatives, rather than a series of disjointed activities. While it's possible to restage a brand without any product upgrades, it's much easier and usually more successful to do so with them.

The core of any brand restage—other than for price brands—should be more and better consumer communications, specifically advertising. You can't justify more advertising media unless you have better advertising creative. As Lesson 4 makes clear, this is why advertising creative is

"New and Improved" Successes

Tide detergent is the classic example of sustained success via repeated rounds of "new and improved" claims. Over the years, Procter & Gamble has run this play literally dozens of times, always reinforcing one central promise: Tide cleans clothes better. At P&G's Copy College, marketers have the importance of superiority claims driven into them over and over. It's so central to their success that Proctoids joke that -er—as in better than—ads are what put the -er in Procter.

It's no joke. In an ocean of me-too brands with largely comparable technology, claims that clearly communicate why consumers should buy your brand in preference to another can be decisive.

Another time-tested way to grow your existing brand is to leave the product as-is but make a new claim based on new research. Many brands have scored share gains by newly communicating that they are now "proven" to be superior to a competitor.

your job number one. Developing great advertising creative is often frustrating, time-consuming, and costly. And it is the area of marketing that top management, legitimately, coaches you on the most. But don't let these factors deter you. The challenges are huge, but so is the payoff. Crack the advertising creative nut, and you are well on your way to transforming your brand.

If you can create winning advertising creative without leveraging new-product news, more power to you. But often, product news serves to break the collective creative block that has kept you and your team from cracking this nut before. As hackneyed as it may seem, adroit communication of "new and improved" is a time-tested brand builder. The key is to have the news or the improvement be on a brand-ownable dimension. The claim should magnify your ongoing brand's point of difference, not dilute it.

In addition to improved advertising creative, successful brand restages include many of the following elements:

- **Incremental media weight**—As mentioned, it takes improved creative to justify increased media. Assuming you have the creative and thus the incremental media dollars, you need to decide how to allocate them. Sometimes your best move is simply to spread the increase evenly across your existing media plan. But often, increased media dollars allow you to add entirely new elements that you simply couldn't afford to consider before. Many brands, for example, have teenagers as secondary targets.

Teens are the point of entry to these brands and categories—and thus critical to future success—but may not be the heaviest users. Increased media levels may also allow an effort targeting Hispanic or African-American consumers. Alternatively, increased media dollars may let a print-only brand make the leap to TV.

- **Packaging improvements**—Your brand's packaging is its silent salesperson. It's on air fifty-two weeks of the year. Make sure you evaluate its selling power regularly, even if you just do so qualitatively. As is the case with advertising, resist mightily the urge to change for change's sake. Having said that, most brands can benefit significantly from an occasional well-directed face-lift. And if you have new news, even if it's just a new fragrance, don't be shy about communicating that on the package as well.

- **A full-throttle sales/customer drive**—Successful restages change the behavior and priorities of your sales force, brokers, and power retailers. Leverage the organizational focus of the restage to fill critical distribution voids, improve your shelf placement, and correct pricing issues. And, remember, the best way to generate awareness and trial of your brand is to get off-shelf displays for it.

- **Product sampling**—Nothing conveys your confidence in your brand's ability to satisfy consumers better than a large-scale sampling program. Pay particular attention to sampling programs such as in-store demonstrations that help to generate incremental off-shelf displays.

Line Extensions

Few issues in the marketing world are more controversial and complex than line extensions. Marketing purists disdain them. They have created a whole bookshelf of arguments against the line-extension trap. Their very well taken point is that line extensions muddy the brand's strategic waters. They reduce the clarity and salience of the brand's positioning. This is why your first focus in growing your brand should be to build it into the dominant brand within its current product category. The risk stemming from line extensions into other categories or segments is that your brand will die from lack of focus.

On the other hand, today's marketing economics make line extensions an unavoidable necessity. The spiraling cost of media is the biggest factor. If a brand isn't growing at near double digits, its inflation-adjusted media budget, and hence awareness and trial levels, will have to shrink. In addition, brands are often forced to spread out to maintain their overall stature as major players—as power retailers demand. The risk stemming from *not* extending your line is that your brand will die from a lack of scale.

In response to these perils, marketers have increasingly employed complex entities variously known as master brands, umbrella brands, subbrands, flanker brands, and the like. The objective is to leverage the existing brand to lower the cost of launching new products, while building the base brand in the process. It's a huge challenge.

In a perfect world, any ad for a given brand would also have a positive halo effect on other products that somehow

Generalities with Halos

There is some evidence that brands with strong, consistent brand characters enjoy broader halos than other brands. L'Oreal is the best mass-market example of this. Its Parisian imagery, upscale models, and the "I'm worth it" theme-line help unify a fairly broad array of products in the beauty category, from cosmetics to shampoo. Estée Lauder, Clinique, and Lancôme have also done a great job of master branding, although in the prestige channels, advertising plays a relatively small role in brand building.

Healthy Choice is a relatively successful master food brand that has a unified consumer end benefit, wrapped up in its brand name. It's not clear how much of this brand's power comes from advertising versus merchandising, however.

Loblaw's, Canada's leading food retailer, has created a brand, President's Choice, unified by its consistently superior taste. This is premium private label at its best. Its marketers smartly focus on categories, such as cookies, where superiority is simply a matter of, say, more chocolate bits. But here again, the advertising is likely not a major driver of success.

also employ the same brand name. We now know—from weekly scanner data—that ad halos are usually very small. Their coverage is limited to the parts of the brand that provide the same key consumer benefit as the advertised product(s). The temptation is to broaden your advertising messages in order to broaden their halo power. But very few generalities sell product.

One of the keys to navigating through this difficult terrain is to build advertisability into your new-product work from the start. Your new-product initiatives need to be large, advertisable chunks of closely related products, not single SKUs and not loosely associated "collections." I call them *chunquities.*

A steady stream of well-executed brand chunquities—some old and some new—carries most successful brands these days. Neutrogena is a master at this. Its marketers have built up for their product a reputation for providing clean, healthy skin, backed by heavy investment in gaining recommendations from dermatologists. The company continues to advertise the original chunquity, the glycerin bar cleanser, but it has also layered in coherently related and sequenced advertisable chunks: moisturizers, acne products, hair care, and cosmetics.

The key advantage of line extensions over new brands doesn't come from advertising efficiencies, from advertising halos. Rather, it comes from an often-overlooked source: merchandising halos. A line extension of a leading brand has a very good chance of piggybacking on off-shelf displays and other merchandising activities already earned and paid for by the parent brand. Similarly, the line extension can take advantage of the parent's favorable shelf position and retail pricing—huge advantages for any product. The merchandising halos also pass from the new product back to the parent. Retailers are as interested in the new as consumers are. A hot new product can earn its parent brand an incremental display—across all its products.

Merchandising efficiencies also accrue to new products that complement their parent brand in some way. For example, a new product that is contra-seasonal to the parent can help justify year-round retailer support for the entire brand. Alternatively, it may have special appeal to certain demographics, such as Hispanics, that help the parent brand gain incremental distribution.

You can maximize merchandising halos by pricing and sizing new products exactly the same as parent products. In addition, you can make any introductory coupons for the new product also good on base products, or you can include a separate coupon at the same time. Some trade-offs are involved, however. You need to be very careful about pricing new products. Introductions are just about your only way to raise your brands' average prices and profit margins today. Power retailers actively resist "normal" price increases. It may be better to provide an introductory allowance on the new product so retailers can line price and line merchandise for the launch period only.

New Brands

Brands that are entirely new to the world are extremely rare. As has been discussed, the media costs and merchan-

Line Extensions: You Make the Call

*Most new products fail, including line extensions. Often
the reasons are obvious. Other times the results seem random. See for yourself if you can find any patterns in the
following list:*

1. *Olay body wash: successful*
2. *Olay Cosmetics: a financial catastrophe despite five
   years of test marketing*
3. *Listerine Oral Care Strips (PocketPacks): ka-ching!*
4. *Listerine toothpaste: a failure each of the many
   times it was tried*
5. *Herbal Essences body wash: yes! yes! yes!*
6. *Herbal Essences body moisturizer: nope*
7. *BIC disposable razor: yes*
8. *BIC fragrances: clunk*
9. *Suave body lotion: yep*
10. *Suave baby care: nope*

dising halos force marketers to piggyback new products on
existing brands unless they have a breakthrough of major
significance. According to IRI, of the top twenty mass-
marketed new chunquities launched in a recent two-year
period, only one is not some sort of line extension. The list
is full of names like Clorox Disinfecting Wipes, Ruffles
Flavor Rush Chips, Mini Oreos, and Cascade Complete.

Physique hair care, the only new-to-the-world brand, was a disaster. Megaflankers are the new brands of the twenty-first century.

The inexorable push away from new brands and toward some sort of master branding is exemplified by Crest White Strips. These represent a real technical innovation with global applicability. The consumer benefit is eminently perceptible. In prior years, this breakthrough certainly would have been the basis for a new brand—or at least the basis for resurrecting the once-strong Gleem brand name. But despite the risk of watering down the parent brand's hard-won health care—"no cavities"—equity, P&G bowed to the need to do a cosmetic flanker.

In truth, there is a glut of brands. The trend is clearly toward fewer, bigger, better. Some companies are actively dropping brands. Others are letting any brand other than global contenders just fade away. Others are forcing several brand equities into one. Mars has changed the name of its U.S. cat food from Crave to Whiskas as part of a global harmonization program. Nestlé has been gradually deemphasizing the Carnation brand in a similar move. Unilever is consolidating numerous value-priced brands into the Suave franchise. The company now sells Rave by Suave, Groom & Clean by Suave, and, in Canada, Pears by Suave.

Creating Successful New Products

With so many issues to consider, how can you create a new product that will succeed? For new-product success, you need the right strategy, a positive culture, insights from consumers themselves, a winning product development team, and careful attention to the financials.

Strategy

All the strategic clarity in the world won't guarantee success in new products. But the lack of it will guarantee failure. Clarity requires that options be identified and hard choices made, at the highest levels of the corporation. The specific new-product strategy—or charter, as it's often called—should come out of a coherent corporate strategy that provides appropriate focus. Marketing, as the voice of the ultimate customer and the keeper of the dominant percentage of discretionary spending, needs to play a leadership role in making the following choices:

- What business are you in? The Great Focusing that consumer product companies have been going through has pretty well answered this for most. The most successful companies can describe their business in a couple of words. L'Oreal is a beauty company. Kraft does food.
- What are or can be your sources of competitive advantage? Be honest!
- How much of your resources should you apply to new products? Again, don't neglect the need to fully establish your existing products.
- In which categories or segments should you focus your new-product work?
- Which geographies should you focus on?

Culture

Much has been written about the need to create a culture that encourages passionate innovation, tolerates risk, and rewards provocation to the status quo. You also need to create a culture that is ruthlessly honest and objective. New products require secrecy for obvious reasons. But within and between the core development and decision-making teams, new-product work requires total transparency.

Consumer Insights

As Lesson 2 stressed, genuine consumer insights are the true coin of the marketing realm. You can create the right environment and apply plenty of resources to come up with that unique, meaningful, believable, and doable insight. But you can't legislate it into existence. After all the labor pains, you

---

Stay Transparent

I once worked for a company with a huge new-product success that was very marketing driven. When the next new product was in development, the marketers kept the sales department and others out of the strategic loop. Success had made them a bit arrogant. Unfortunately, they missed several key caution flags, and the result was a major failure. More transparency among functions would have helped them make the proposition better or, at least, would have made them more aware of its weaknesses.

---

either have a baby or you don't. Whatever you do, don't let an unrealistic timetable force you to compromise on the critical step of discovering a leverageable insight. And don't fall into the trap of rationalizing that you can make an insight that is just OK work because the execution is superlative.

The Team

New-product development, like advertising development, is a team sport. Here are some tips to make sure you have a winning team.

Keep reminding yourself, "It's the leader, stupid." Established brands can get away with suboptimal leadership for a while. The team can coast on prior initiatives and strategies. Repeating past programs can still yield decent results. But new products go absolutely nowhere without the real thing—the true monomaniac on a mission. In addition to having focus, passion, and creativity, the team leader also needs to be an accomplished and respected grower of established brands. I have never seen an isolated new-products group succeed. The team simply must be connected to the real world of sales and profits. This is even truer in the age of power retailers, the world's best new-product consultants.

All functions need to be represented on the team, at least virtually. To function effectively, the core new-product team needs to be relatively small—a brand marketer leader, marketing researcher, product developer, financial planner, packaging expert, and eventually an ad agency person. In addition, you must systematically get input and buy-in from many other areas without wasting their time or the core team's time in day-to-day discussions. Identify who these key stakeholders are, copy them on the minutes, and include them in your major quarterly checkpoint meetings.

Get an executive sponsor. Occasionally new product can be successfully developed via a bottom-up process, assuming the overall corporate growth strategy is clear. But in most cases, having a top executive with skin in the game is essential. This sponsor provides a thirty-thousand-foot perspective that the core team can't possibly have. He or she can also clear hurdles, assure resources, and smooth out the bumps that all new products hit along the way. And most important, you need someone with a personal investment in the project in the room when the big go/no go decision is made. No matter how much research you conduct, new-product launches are always risky calls, with lots of room for interpretation.

Financials

One of the reasons new-to-the-world brand launches have become so scarce is that companies have gotten much better at understanding the total system costs involved. Even for moderate-sized line extensions, the costs are very high. This is why it's critical to have a finance person on the core new-product team right from the start.

Typically, manufacturers shoot for breaking even on a contribution margin basis in three years, cumulatively. So, a new product may lose $5 million in its first year, come in at about breakeven in its second year, and then make $5 million in its third year—if it's successful. Keep in mind that this does not include any fixed costs or any technology and marketing development costs. You also need to factor in cannibalization of your other products' sales. If you are launching a product that is one hundred percent complementary to your existing products—that is, it has zero cannibalization from the standpoint of consumer appeal—there will still be trade cannibalization. Trade cannibalization takes the form of reduced sales force attention, reduced merchandising, and possibly reduced shelving. The final cost is opportunity cost. How much more profit could you have made if the time, personnel, and financial resources invested in the new product had been spent on existing products?

Because of the huge financial consequences and the general level of uncertainty, make sure you master the fine art of the throwaway schedule. This is especially important for capitalized costs, which can affect the company for years, even if the project is shut down.

The Brand Name

A brand, at its most basic level, is a name. A great brand name should be short, easy to pronounce, and evocative of the product category and/or the product benefit you intend to communicate. Tide, Wisk, Secret, Curél, and Finesse are classic examples. As media clutter has increased, slightly more descriptive names have become more popular. We chose the name Salon Selectives for a salon-heritage brand that offered customized hair care because the name was the claim. But don't get too descriptive, or you risk being generic and unmemorable. The brand graveyard is full of names like these.

Developing and protecting a trademark-able brand name, subbrand name, packaging design, logo style, and other intellectual property rights is one of your central responsibilities. It's also one of the toughest. Trademarks can literally make or break a brand. Until 1990 or so, a costly trademark shell game was played in which all the major consumer product companies created a name bank of potential trademarks that had the legal fig leaf of having had token shipments made across state lines. Although these token shipments didn't really protect the trademarks, they created enough uncertainty among competitors that many good names were kept off the market. Current trademark law requires a bona fide intent to use and clearly excludes token shipments from qualifying. Progress.

But now, with the explosion of new channels, especially the Internet, many good names are owned by small companies that are fully legitimate but may have revenues of only hundreds of dollars. Often, the best way to get the mark you want in these cases is to buy it from its owner through a third party. If necessary, you can license the name back to the previous owner (even on a royalty-free basis), with channel limitations, so the previous owner

(continued)

doesn't have to change its labels. If, as is sometimes the case, several small companies are using a mark you want, buy them all out—or at least all that have a semblance of first-use rights.

Be aggressive in obtaining legal rights, and be aggressive in defending them. Regardless of the legal counsel you get, remember it is just that, counsel. You are the line manager responsible for either making the decision or moving it up the corporate hierarchy to the level where it can be made. Don't make the mistake of caving on a legal issue just because you don't want to deal with your management on the issue.

The New-Product Launch

Congratulations, you've got a new product ready to launch. You've got a distinctive consumer insight that has led to good direction for R&D, packaging, and the ad agency. Launch plans have been prepared and approved, and top management has given the thumbs up. Now the fun really begins.

The marketplace handoff between marketing and sales, like any birthing process, is difficult. You have assiduously involved headquarters salespeople in the development of your initiatives and perhaps participated directly in consultative sales calls with key retailers. Still, there is always a significant risk that your baby, your new-product initiative that you and your team have labored over for a minimum of nine months, will get twisted up in its umbilical cord. Much can be lost twixt the cup and the lip. Don't let it happen to your new product.

The most problematic friction between sales and marketing is lead time. Power retailers are commercial aircraft carriers. They don't turn on a dime. Consumer product manufacturers now need to be presenting new initiatives to them a full nine months (or more) before expected in-store implementation. This nine-month lead time compares to the traditional two- to three-month lead time required by the small food retailer of old. Even when the marketing function does its job flawlessly and provides fully for this lead time, there is an ever-present risk that management will decide to accelerate the launch, to strike while the iron is hot, or to preempt a just-uncovered competitive threat. Often the pressure to move the timing forward comes directly from top management, but it also may come from the sales and marketing functions themselves. Speed thrills, but it also kills. All worship the ideal of doing it right the first time. It takes a very broad, experienced eye and a full-system perspective to make these key timing calls.

A big part of the timing problem stems from the schedules around which power retailers revise their planograms. For advertised new products, you have no choice but to line up your launch dates with the time frames your key retailers use to update their shelf plans. Otherwise, you are liable to commit one of the cardinal sins of marketing: advertising to empty shelves.

The Power Brand Exception

Every once in a while, a new-product launch will be big enough to force retailers to be totally flexible. When Gillette launches a once-a-decade update of its shaving system, the company can expect full retailer participation, regardless of when the products start shipping. When P&G decided to change all its laundry detergent packaging and formulas, as happened a few years ago with the move to concentrated Ultra, retailers fell in line, especially since this move freed up shelf space. But, remember, these are exceptions to the rule.

Even if you fully acknowledge the need to tie in with shelf-set dates, there is no easy timing answer. Retailers change their minds often, and they are never in sync with each other. The relative consistency of Wal-Mart's updates, plus its size and growth, ends up being the decisive factor in many cases. This is one of the retail giant's quiet competitive advantages since it ensures Wal-Mart has optimum in-store conditions when the heavy introductory brand support is taking place.

The Sales Meeting

Sales meetings are yet another activity that has been dramatically changed by power retailers. Your biggest customers don't want glossy sales pitches. They want senior management to consult with them on the development of the new product and consult with them on the actual launch. This all happens before most of your (smaller) retail customers are even ready to think about next year. Eventually, after you have sold to the buyers representing perhaps 70 percent of your volume, your company will hold a big national meeting.

It's important to realize this isn't really a sales meeting; it's a company meeting. Certainly, you will get your chance to increase your personal stature in the organization by pulling off your part. More importantly, you will help write the scripts for your entire organization. CFOs and CEOs will use your slides in analyst and shareholder meetings. R&D, operations, marketing research, and other functions will get the feeling that all the sometimes mind-numbing work was worth it. If your agency hasn't delivered the goods yet, they'll certainly get a fire lit underneath them. Well-executed sales meetings are truly group hugs. Along the way, the salespeople and brokers calling on the small retailers will be fully armed to get those few extra points of distribution that can make or break a launch.

CMO Checkpoints

1. Don't neglect the need to fully establish your promising existing products. They are still new to most consumers.
2. Organize your advertising spending around chunks of products with similar benefits. Recognize that your creative will not have a halo much beyond them.

3. Merchandising halos can be quite big, especially if you pay attention to issues like line pricing and sizing.
4. Consider new-to-the-world brands only if you have a profoundly powerful consumer insight matched to a product that delivers fully on its promise.
5. Successful new-product work requires crystal-clear strategic direction, marketing leadership that is tightly linked to the existing business, a high-performance cross-functional core team, a top-management sponsor, and great financial acumen.
6. Involve power retailers early and often.
7. Recognize that your new-product sales meeting is really a total company meeting.

Lesson 8

Financial Optimization

Consumer product marketers need to be financial leaders as well as marketing leaders. While demand creation is your key role, no other function in your company—not finance, not sales, and not even top management—is in a better position to manage the big-picture economics of your brand. This responsibility for the bottom line is what has made marketing the training ground for the executive suite at consumer product companies. Managing the money can also be one of the most interesting parts of your job.

Make the Numbers Your Friends

Finance is the lingua franca of business. Ultimately, everything can be reduced to such financial measures as return on investment, economic value added, or market value.

Make sure you put in a good effort to become fluent in finance-speak.

As a starting point, make sure you fully grasp the underlying financial drivers of your industry. For most businesses, advances in communication and computation technology have led to a massive shift toward globalization and its handmaiden, consolidation. To thrive in this environment, almost every company, even the giant ones, have been forced to become more focused on the relatively few product and competency areas in which they can be world class. This has greatly shortened the list of key, direct competitors. Know these competitors stone cold. Know their market values (stock price times number of shares outstanding) as well as you know your own company's. Know their sources of competitive advantage and key strategic thrusts.

This macro view will help you place your specific brand and category battles in the right perspective. For example, you need to know what strategic role your brand or category is expected to play in your corporation's overall portfolio. Most fundamentally, is the mission mostly about sales growth or profit delivery? No marketer wants to be on a brand that's being milked to fund growth of a star business. Your job is to lead the generation of initiatives that will create high growth. But again, you need to know the industry and corporate context in which you operate in order to either sell your high-growth plan or know, alternatively, when it's time to accept your role of cranking out maximum profits. This knowledge also helps you target your brand assignments, to the extent that's under your control.

The three- or five-year plans that you and your team put together and ultimately get approval for sketch out the financial blueprint and underlying assumptions for your brand. Your annual plan fills in the many details. Two parts of this blueprint are critically important. First, the income statement, often called the profit and loss statement (P&L), includes information on sales and expenses. Second, the balance sheet contains information on capitalized assets. Of course, the major way to affect your financials is to increase sales by stimulating consumer demand. But to do so, you need to understand the fundamentals of finance that will help you capture the maximum economic gain from each dollar of sales.

Profit Margins

The margin structure of a product is largely set long before the first case ships—when the product's basic specifications (specs) are being set. It's imperative that you get this right the first time. If you and your team have done your homework, you will have margin targets clearly laid out in your new-products charter.

In most cases, new products should have profit margins that are higher than the brand or company averages. Here's why:

- Most new products involve significant risk. Higher risk requires higher expected returns.

- New products create at least some cannibalization of existing products. Even if consumers don't trade over, retailers very well may trade off shelf space or merchandising—indirectly leading to consumer cannibalization.
- Even the most sophisticated accounting practices inevitably miss some of the soft or hidden costs that are required for new products. These costs include top management and sales force attention, not to mention substantial opportunity costs, such as the diversion of attention from the established brands.

Make sure the margin targets you are shooting for are the correct ones. For simple line extensions, which don't require many fixed marketing expenses, focusing on the direct product margin (revenues minus cost of goods sold) is usually enough. For heavily marketed flankers or new brands, you need to go further down the P&L and look at margins after marketing. This can get very tricky when some of the marketing is not truly incremental (since some of the base brand marketing is being reallocated to new products). At a minimum, you need to make these considerations visible. A good way to do this is simply to run several P&L versions that show the fully allocated as well as the partially allocated scenarios.

One of the biggest challenges with new products is completing accurate cost estimates on a timely basis. Top management won't approve a proposal without fully developed cost estimates, but the operations and accounting groups are loath to do the painstaking work needed to provide estimates on unapproved projects. Most organizations have developed a process for getting quick and dirty cost estimates as a way around this catch-22. If your organization doesn't have a process for quickly running order-of-magnitude costing estimates, establish one. If used with discipline and professional rigor, these estimates can work well. The risk is that you ask for too many estimates and that operations and accounting build in such conservative guesstimates that nothing moves ahead. To push through, you need judgment, experience, internal benchmarking, tenacity, and good working relationships.

You will face ongoing profit margin pressures even if the specs for the initial launch are optimal. Your sales force and ad agencies will make sure you are fully aware that competition is heating up. Brand X has a larger market or trade development fund. Brand Y just doubled its coupon values. Brand Z has a huge Hispanic ad campaign. Input costs, especially media rates but also cost of goods sold, almost always go up. The shareholders will demand an ever-bigger piece of flesh. Here are some margin-enhancing tools at your disposal:

- Grow your brand! Without a doubt, leadership brands are more profitable. They get better distribution, better shelving, better merchandising support, and hotter pricing.
- Save money where you spend money. Work on every line of the P&L, but focus on the half dozen or so lines that really count.

- Eliminate differences that don't differentiate. Almost every new product comes out with some feature that turns out to be less of a reason to buy than originally envisioned.
- Fix the mix. Lean into higher-margin SKUs in terms of marketing support and distribution priority.
- Exploit interrelationships. Many cost savings can be generated only by working across several brands, functions, or even divisions.
- Leverage scale and certainty. Systematically go back to each vendor and ask for price breaks now that you are a real, growing, in-market product or brand. Dangle long-term commitments.
- "Operationalize" the product. Even in the best-run new-product launches, there is often too little time for the operations functions to add all the value they can. Just chairing meetings between R&D and operations can yield huge postlaunch savings.
- Avoid the temptation to overproliferate, especially special packs. Although it is hard to quantify, complexity is expensive. Keep it simple.
- Celebrate margin improvements as a way to reward people and encourage further results. Unlike breakthrough technology or advertising, most major cost-savings programs involve many, many people, including hourly employees. These successes are ideal for writing up in the company newsletter and showcasing at companywide meetings.

Staffing for Cost Control

Very few marketers are equally good at or enjoy being all the spokes of the wheel. Some are better at the conceptual, intuitive, and creative side of the job, while others are much better at the nuts and bolts of the operational side. Overall brand health requires strong capabilities in all areas. Recognizing the importance of developmental assignments and the need for brand rotations, at some point many marketers need to be channeled into some degree of specialization. If your organization is light on margin mavens, you may need to consider reallocating some head count to beef up your operations expertise. At Helene Curtis, we created a subdepartment called Marketing Operations just to make sure this area of the business got enough attention. Other companies have created a hybrid role called project management to help. Margin management needs to be managed.

Pricing Strategies

For almost every consumer product category, one of the top two market segmentation dimensions is pricing. In fact, if you see a segmentation scheme that doesn't have either the x- or the y-axis labeled "pricing," watch out. Most categories now have more price segments than benefit segments, especially when you factor in the prestige and specialty channels of distribution. In facial moisturizer, for example, you can pay $3 for a bottle of a private-label brand, $4 for a value brand such as Suave, $7 for a standard mass-market brand, $18 for a premium subbrand of a mass-market brand such as Olay Total Effects, $25 for a lower-end department store brand such as Clinique, or $50 for a premium department store brand such as Lancôme. Work this source of potential differentiation hard. Yes, pricing *can* be a creative area.

Neutral Pricing

Most large consumer product companies have historically had the same, undifferentiated pricing strategy. It's been such a given that it's seldom articulated to anybody by anybody. Here's that silent strategy: make pricing a neutral issue. Think about it. How is the pricing strategy on Crest differentiated from that used on Colgate? Is Pepsi priced differently from Coke? How about Pampers versus Huggies? Or Folgers versus Maxwell House? The answer is that all these brands are priced in the neutral zone.

The basic rationale for this plain-vanilla approach to pricing is that it keeps things simple. It frees up resources that can be applied to more sustainable points of differentiation. It makes test marketing or concept testing more valid since consumers have one less variable to process. It allows the sales force to concentrate on the brand benefits rather than getting into a difficult pricing conversation with retailers.

Premium Pricing

For the most part, stable, neutral pricing works quite well for unembattled incumbents. The problem is, there are hardly any unembattled incumbents anymore. You now need to explore many pricing options. Challenger brands and companies often can generate real marketplace traction by avoiding the neutral pricing zone. L'Oreal's strategy of coming in slightly above the vanilla pricing line set by the dominant incumbent is an outstanding example of the premium approach ("Because I'm worth it"). L'Oreal has been so successful with this strategy, the brand has taken over category leadership in many areas and forced Bristol-Myers Squibb to sell Clairol to P&G. Similarly, Beiersdorf of Germany has gone the high road with brands like Nivea and Eucerin. Niche players in beer, such as Sam Adams and most imports, also have taken the premium-pricing road to success.

Even strong incumbent brands are adding, or trying to add, premium subbrands. Secret deodorant now has the successful Secret Platinum. Old Spice has Old Spice High Endurance and, more recently, Old Spice High Endurance Red Zone. Many food brands, such as Campbell's in soup, have added some sort of "select" premium subline. In these cases, high pricing is actually part of the benefit bundle the consumer is buying—a signal of quality.

Low-Road Pricing

Challenging incumbents by taking the low road on pricing also is becoming more common. Although many people look down at these so-called bottom feeders, they are an essential part of the creative destruction process that the consumer product industry runs on. If the premium brands rest on their value-added laurels—that is, if they let their product technology or consumer insights get stale—they can and do lose share to lower-priced brands. And that is how it should be.

Unilever's relative strength in huge, developing markets such as India has nudged it strategically in the direction of focusing on low cost and low price. This focus is sometimes referred to as its "everyman" strategy. Colgate's historical strength in many developing markets (and weakness in many categories in developed markets) has had a similar impact. Even P&G, a late mover in the globalization battle, is now being forced to work the lower end of the market in the developing world. For the most part, these companies wisely avoid using their premium brand names and thus avoid the issue of global retailers demanding the lowest worldwide price for all their markets. What's in play here is the need to achieve fully competitive critical mass in all key geographies, even if it means leveraging economies of manufacturing and distribution more than skill in marketing and formulation. Another factor is the need to be cost-competitive with emerging, low-cost, local manufacturers such as T-Joy of China and Amul of India.

The need for huge consumer product companies to compete in two strategic domains (differentiation in the developed world and cost focus in the developing one) makes their business significantly more complex. If they manage to win in both, look to them to focus more aggressively on the lower-priced part of the market in developed economies as well—up to and including private label.

Pricing on Acquired and New Brands

Acquisitions also have nudged consumer product companies toward a more varied pricing approach. Sometimes nonneutral pricing is a key reason for the acquisition in the first place, such as P&G's acquisition of superpremium Iams pet food. But often the disparate price point just comes with a purchase made for other reasons. P&G got the then superpremium-priced Pantene when it bought the Richardson-Vicks health care business. Unilever bought Chesebrough Ponds for its skin care but also got low-priced Rave hair spray in the same deal.

More recently, the major players have started to launch their own new-to-the-world brands at very unusual (for them) prices. Estée Lauder went way down in price when launching Jane Cosmetics into the mass market (low even for the mass market). P&G's first new-to-the-world haircare brand in over twenty years, Physique, was launched at pricing dramatically higher than anything on the mass market.

Pricing has always been a central part of the marketing mix, although for many years it was a relatively quiet part of it. No more. Going forward, you need to work through the many pricing options as thoroughly as you work the product, advertising, and packaging ones.

Changing Prices

In the seventies and eighties, when inflation was much higher than it is today, price changes occurred quite frequently. In fact, it was once possible to use pricing as an introductory trial device for new products because marketers could take a price increase in year two, after achieving trial objectives. Not now. More than ever, the price you launch with is the price you will need to live with for a long time.

Even so, pricing is never a static variable. Things change. Competitors take increases or rollbacks on existing brands or launch entirely new ones. Retail customers come up with new approaches to pricing and merchandising. New research methods are developed for modeling price changes. Your advertising gets less or, hopefully, more compelling. Product and packaging technology progresses. Shareholder demands increase. New management comes in. All of these create the need for tactical modifications. Pricing is never done.

Components of Pricing

Pricing is not just about your price. You need to think of your trade promotions, coupons, and other sources of discounts (such as scale and cash allowances) as part of your pricing. Pricing is also about your relative sizing, both on open stock and bonus pack sizes if you have them. In some cases, consumers clearly think in terms of price per package or price per ounce. In others, the absolute price point is dominant in their perception of a brand. In most cases, it's a complicated blend of all of these factors. The consumer is the boss, and pricing needs to be understood as the consumer's net perception.

Pricing is never about just one price, either. There's everyday shelf price, promoted price, blended average price. And, of course, these are different for every class of trade (and customer), and they change over time. They even change within a specific retailer on the same brand in different geographies. For a variety of reasons, including transportation costs and relative competitive intensity, retailers in the Northwest, for instance, charge more for every brand.

The tactical complexity of pricing is one of the reasons it makes sense to hire, train, and empower salespeople who can truly act like the customer business managers they are now often called. You need to set national guidelines and financial controls, but you can't and shouldn't try to be involved in day-to-day, customer-specific pricing tactics.

Price Increases

It's your fiduciary responsibility to lead the charge for price increases. At Alberto-Culver, our approach was to require each brand/sales team to justify why it was not proposing an annual price increase, rather than the other way around. The default action was to take a price increase. Especially if you are the market or segment leader, you need to push hard on these. Remember to fix the roof when the sun is shining—that is, it's easiest to pass through a price increase when your brand is on a legitimate roll, driven by consumer demand. Even if you have to price up and then dial back the increase for the short term with promotional activity, the long-run benefits are considerable. Just run the math and see how many margin points you can pick up with a nominal price increase.

Several analytic tools have been developed to help inform your pricing decisions, particularly scanner-data-based elasticity studies. However, as previously mentioned, these are very expensive. On small brands, the studies can cost more than the price increase can generate in incremental profit. Your resources are usually better spent working with your sales and finance people to dig deep on the impact of contemplated price changes at your top five to seven customers.

You need to look at key competitors, of course, but also at the relative importance of everyday pricing versus promotional pricing. Most importantly, you need to judge the relative clout of your brand. Retailers take lower margins on key battleground categories such as milk and liters of soda in order to make their own marketing statement and to attract traffic. They also take lower margins on some leadership brands. If you have a top brand in a big category that is growing rapidly, you very well may be able to take a reasonable price increase that the retailers simply eat, meaning they don't pass it on to consumers. This is one of those cases where size really does matter. But be careful about the possible harm this could do to your second-tier brand or brands, especially those in the same category. Retail buyers keep company scorecards as well as brand scorecards. One way or another, they will push to make their margin goals.

Be particularly careful about going above promotional trigger-price thresholds. For example, most brands will sell a lot more just below a certain whole-dollar level—say, $2.99—than they will just above it—say, $3.19. Even if consumer take-away declines only slightly, this may put you below the minimum sales level retailers require to include you in their key merchandising vehicles, such as end-cap displays. Unfortunately, this is a pass/fail situation; you are either in all the way or out all the way. In addition, be careful about the margin spring-load effect. Retailers may have been taking a thin margin on you before to achieve trigger promotion prices. If you push the price up too much, they may swing the other way. Your 5 percent increase could end up looking to consumers like a 10 or 12 percent increase.

Price Increases via Size Reductions

Often it's tempting to go for a size reduction (to increase the price per ounce) rather than an outright price increase. But keep the total systems costs in mind when considering this. In addition to the possible capital costs and the hard inventory costs, there are numerous (sometimes hidden) costs at the customer level. In addition, the increasing tightness of the overall product supply system provides less sizing flexibility than even a few years ago. When we slightly downsized even as big a brand as Suave hair care a few years ago, it flowed through the system with few glitches.

We didn't need to change the UPC. You just can't do that anymore. And changes in UPCs lead to slotting allowances. You should also be aware that several state governments make a point of discouraging price increases via downsizing. They are concerned this can mislead consumers.

Today, even down-weighting (selling the same amount of product in a lighter-weight package) is a problem. Several major retailers, including Kroger and Meijers, are installing self-checkout systems, where consumers scan their own products with no involvement from store personnel. In these systems, the exact weight of the product—including the weight of the package—is as critical as the UPC.

Asset Management

Aggressive margin management, including smart pricing decisions, can do a lot to increase the financial yield of each dollar of sales you are able to generate on your brand. But a marketer also can have a profound impact on the balance sheet. To do this involves moving away from sales, expenses, and profits to asset management—or capital management, as it's also called. There are two broad classes of assets: fixed assets and working assets.

Fixed Assets

Occasionally, especially when launching new products, you will be involved in capital purchases. Most of these purchases will be relatively small, such as $40,000 for a new package mold. Others may involve capacity planning or

Line Pricing

One variable you should pay particular attention to is line pricing. All other things being equal, it's nice to line-price many SKUs or groups of SKUs together. This makes it easier for retailers to execute such promotions as end-cap displays and feature ads. But in most—though not all—instances, line pricing leaves a lot of money on the table. Only a third of even the most heavily promoted brands and categories are actually sold with the help of any retail merchandising. For many brands and categories, the figure is under 5 percent. The rest are sold at regular price from the regular shelf location, without a feature ad or even a temporary price reduction.

Set your pricing based on how most of your products are actually sold. And keep in mind that retailers really don't need to have exactly the same pricing on different SKUs in order to promote them together. They can blend the pricing across SKUs. They can also make the math work to hit their overall margin targets by managing how much they lower the promotion price relative to how aggressive they are with everyday pricing.

entire new manufacturing lines that can easily get into the tens of millions of dollars. In any event, be prepared for shockingly low authority to approve capital expenditures. This is one area in which CFOs maintain a very tight grip.

And don't think that an approved annual capital plan means anything is approved. When it comes to financial scrutiny, just be thankful normal marketing expenses aren't capitalized.

Whenever you can, avoid the need for new capital. Walk the lines with your manufacturing counterpart. Find out his or her wish list regarding marketing specifications. Perhaps you can agree on a minor change that will speed up production but will not be detectable by consumers. For example, if you go with an opaque or even translucent package instead of transparent, you may not need to overfill the package to make it look better. Besides speeding the filling process, this may reduce your cost of goods sold.

Make sure you have scoured your company's molds and dies, as well as your manufacturing change parts, around the world. For example, can you just modify that old package mold they used to use in Germany, rather than create an entirely new mold? Again, challenge your assumptions about what the market really calls for. In many instances, there is a range of acceptable options. This is yet another area where a high-performing cross-functional team can really help. There's no substitute for informed, iterative, cross-functional exchange. And, as is the case in so many other areas of the consumer product business, marketing needs to provide the leadership.

Working Capital

Your primary impact on your corporation's capital base results from your ability (or inability) to accurately forecast demand for your brand or brands. Forecast accuracy is directly related to the amount of inventory you have to carry. Even with all the system-based tools available, including historical sales by customer by SKU by month by distribution center, forecasting continues to be a weakness at most consumer product companies. Forecasting is where you find yourself planted firmly between the rock of excess inventory (undersold) and the hard place of out-of-stocks (oversold). Your goal is to substitute information for inventory.

Even though a good portion of most consumer product companies' retail customer base gives them full visibility to day-by-day, store-by-store, SKU-by-SKU sales, you can't turn that into a national demand forecast. The challenge is to take this fairly predictable demand base and add in everything else. You have to add the fairly predictable composite base of smaller retailers plus the very unpredictable promotional quantities and distribution gains (and losses) of your top customers. And that's not to mention the impact of advertising, couponing, competitive factors, and other marketing or environmental factors.

Because the impact, particularly the promotional impact, of power retailers is so great, many consumer product companies are trying to get the sales function more involved in forecasting. One unexpected promotional order from Wal-Mart can destroy the quality of your service to all other customers. On the other hand, one unexpected distribution loss there can force you to carry a year or more of inventory of that item.

The problem with having people in sales responsible for forecasting is that they seldom have the tools or training for it, and they generally hate doing it. If the sales department creates a subfunction to handle forecasting, those people quickly become just another staff group that is just as dependent on the short-of-time field sales force as any other staff group would be. But at least they have a common boss who can insist that the fields' performance objectives be based on accurate forecasts.

Assuming your sales department assigns some dedicated people to forecasting, the marketing function should be able to take their forecast as-is for the near term (say, a quarter) and make judgments (with sales input) for the out quarters. Then marketing should be able to feed these inputs, along with expense projections, into the financial planning group to derive a fairly accurate, up-to-date P&L. I wish it were that simple.

Unless there are massive incentive overrides, the institutional bias of the sales organization is to make so much product that salespeople will never have to sit, red-faced, with a retail customer and explain why they have back-ordered or short-shipped product. To a lesser extent, this is also the bias of marketing, since the cost of capital created by excess inventory is inevitably buried in some overhead line far below the brand profit line they are responsible for. The CFO and others in top management are highly sensitive to wasting cash on excess inventory (and their bonuses are usually tied to return on investment or economic value added, not just P&L performance). Still, they are also desperate not to leave any sales on the table by creating service problems.

The key to improving forecasting is to agree on major overall metrics, including both high-level metrics, such as customer satisfaction and inventory turnover, and the more bite-sized, day-to-day metrics, such as a week's supply of inventory targets and order fill rates. A cross-functional reengineering team, led by someone in the sales function

SKU Pruning

Pruning your SKU count is the surest route to greater forecasting accuracy. Start with setting minimum thresholds for SKU size, then actively kill new-product candidates that don't have a good chance of making the threshold. Aggressively discontinue substandard existing SKUs, working closely with sales to ensure that the distribution slots are filled with another of the company's SKUs. And guard against too many special packs and too much customization. Sometimes, the financial algebra is so complicated that total system costs of an initiative can't be accurately determined with the resources you have available. A handy shortcut is simply to be empirical, that is, study what your bigger competitors have done and assume they have done their homework.

with heavy involvement from key people in marketing, information systems, and finance, needs to be assembled at least once every couple of years to take another whack at this never-ending business challenge.

Because the gross margins in most consumer product businesses are so high, often in the range of 70 or even 80 percent, there is huge operating leverage. This means you can dramatically improve your financial results just by growing sales at a relatively modest rate. Thus, sale growth deservedly gets the most airtime in any discussion of results. At the same time, however, persistent attention to basics of margin and asset management, especially pricing and forecasting, can make the difference between good and great. Make sure you keep a focus here.

CMO Checkpoints

1. Financial leadership is a key part of every marketer's job. Embrace it. Make the numbers your friend.
2. Good margins begin at the design phase of new products. Have margin goals up front, and do it right the first time.
3. Treat introductory pricing strategies as a creative endeavor. Make them a source of competitive advantage.
4. Don't leave money on the table through nonessential line pricing.

5. Don't ask why you should take a price increase. Explain why you shouldn't.
6. Abhor capital investments. Search for previously used equipment and molds. Refit old tools. Improvise.
7. Reduce working capital through forecasting diligence and sharp SKU pruning.

Global Marketing

U p till about 1990, there was still serious debate about whether or not the consumer product industry was heading for full globalization, along the lines of the auto and electronics industries. Unilever was still clinging to its multilocal strategy in which country managers held the decisive power over the "coordinators" of global category and brand strategy. The international divisions of many consumer companies were unprofitable career eddies. Suppliers were almost all local. Retailers were overwhelmingly focused on one or two countries. Although even back then, marketers were urged to "Think globally, act locally," the reality was more along the lines of "Budget globally, think and act locally."

The debate on globalization goes on today. But now it revolves around whether or not globalization is an unmitigated good thing. The protests at international economic gatherings is a part of this. But full globalization of consumer products is here, without debate.

Strategic Consequences of Globalization

The Information Revolution has made the full globalization of consumer product companies possible and inevitable, but global marketing is still very difficult to do well. It adds an entire vector of strategic and tactical complexity to any organization. It requires cultural change. It is, to use an overused buzzword in its proper context, a major paradigm shift.

The strategic skeleton of every company's business plan consists of what the company sells, what channel customers its products and services are sold to, and what geographies it sells into. If the geographical axis gets bigger and more varied, you have no choice but to simplify either what you sell, which channels you sell through, or both. At the same time, you need to work hard to keep any geographical expansion as simple and coherent as possible.

When the global marketing gold rush began in earnest, the easiest strategic choice that consumer product companies made was to dump noncore industries. Procter & Gamble got out of pulp paper. Colgate got out of health care. Kao got out of floppy disks. Henkel got out of chemicals. Dial got out of buses. Ralston Purina got out of farm products. General Mills got out of restaurants. Unilever got out of fragrances. Many of these jettisoned operations were vertical integration carryovers that were highly suspect even before global markets opened up. Globalization just provided the final shove.

Another easy strategic choice consumer companies have made in response to global markets has been to prune their marketing channels. P&G and Unilever got out of prestige channels (department stores) to focus on the mass market exclusively. Gillette got out of door-to-door sales (Jafra Cosmetics). Lots of food companies have sold off their institutional food service distribution companies.

Much tougher decisions are those that force companies to drop noncore categories or brands within their core industry sector and channels. Crisco, one of P&G's first products, was made from the same raw material used for Ivory soap. It was a tough call for P&G to get out of this brand and other food areas, including peanut butter and baked goods. S. C. Johnson, after a strong track record of profitable innovation in personal care, was forced to focus on its household product business in order to remain globally viable. Dial did the same thing, although in Dial's case, cutting back was the only way the company could remain viable even on a domestic level. Anheuser-Busch was forced to give up on salty snacks to focus on its increasingly global core beer business.

Recently, some consumer product companies have gone the next logical step and started pruning noncore functions even within their main businesses. Any function, any department that is not deemed to be a core competency required to win in the chosen businesses is subject to outsourcing. Most consumer product companies are now outsourcing much of their sales function to brokers. Advertising creative is almost always outsourced. A recent trend is to outsource traditional in-house work, such as the human resources function. P&G is in the process of outsourcing thousands of back-office administrative jobs in a bold experiment in going virtual.

Having fewer industries, channels, categories, brands, and functions to deal with can greatly facilitate global success. Figuring out how much pruning is appropriate takes a clear-eyed view of your relative competitive strength. Selecting targets for cutbacks requires an equally clear-eyed view of your true sources of competitive advantage.

Selecting Businesses to Expand Geographically

A critical step in your globalization process is selection of the specific products to focus on. This requires that you first select the category in which you have the most sustainable competitive advantage. The second step is to select the specific brand or brands within that category.

Category Selection

The overarching strategic priority of any consumer product company is to establish global viability in at least one meaningful product category. This is the core of the core. Gillette in razor blades. Colgate in toothpaste. L'Oreal in beauty care. Hershey in chocolate. Kellogg's in cereal. Kimberly Clark in diapers. It is far better to be like the hedgehog that can win in one thing than the fox that can fritter away its time in many categories, while lacking leadership or near leadership in any of them.

Usually, the category to select for global expansion is obvious. It's the one in which the company has the most sales. Size or critical mass is a pretty good surrogate for competitive advantage. But not always. You can have a lot of sales in a category, even highly profitable sales, and still be strategically marginal in that category. Perhaps it is simply a huge category or one in which you have only a small global share. Unilever has a billion-dollar global fabric-care business that is so dwarfed by P&G's that it is completely marginal. Unilever has been reduced to totally derivative brands like Surf versus Tide. Unilever's problem is not that it is not as good at marketing as P&G. Rather, the company is not playing with a full deck in the fabric-care category. In personal cleansing—that is, soap—P&G plays the fool to Unilever's dominant market share.

Global market share is a better indicator of competitive advantage than absolute sales, but it also can be misleading. Sometimes the category is just structurally unattractive, meaning it's a low-return business at almost any share. There just may not be much opportunity to add value through either technology or image building. Or perhaps a category solves a problem or meets a need that is receding. A good example of this is the antidandruff shampoo seg-

Technology Travels

A great example of the fact that technology travels is P&G's global rollout of its proprietary two-in-one shampoo-plus-conditioner technology. The idea of a two-in-one blend of shampoo and conditioner has been around for years. Revlon once had a brand called Milk Plus Six positioned as a two-in-one, but the product's performance was poor. By 1987 P&G had developed numerous patented process and formulation technologies that allowed the company to deliver on the positioning promise. Ed Artz, then P&G's chairman, forced the world's first hyperspeed rollout of a consumer product technology. He didn't worry about marketing niceties like having a common brand name. The product was called Pert Plus in the United States, Vidal Sassoon Wash & Go in much of Europe, and either Rejoy or Rejoice in much of Asia. Artz didn't worry about building manufacturing capabilities before launch, either. The focus was on getting the bottles on the shelf in every retailer in the world and on getting mailed or hand-delivered samples to every consumer in the world.

A couple of years later, the same technology was applied to a more unified and even more successful global launch, Pantene Pro V. Although the two-in-one feature was mentioned on the packaging, the brand was eventually positioned as a superconditioning shampoo that was to be used with a superconditioning conditioner for supe-

*rior health and shine. Today, Pantene Pro V's global sales
are well above $1 billion.*

*In contrast to the cross-border appeal of technology is
the failure of low-price strategies to travel well. Low price
is the easiest way for local companies to compete against
the global players. A low-price strategy requires a minimum of overhead for advertising or technology development. In addition, many local companies are privately
held and thus can meet their owner's objectives with lower
returns than can publicly traded companies. But even if a
market-leading low-price brand is owned by a major
player, it's hard to launch it in other countries. Retailers,
the real marketers of price brands, don't want to drive
down profits with an additional low-price entrant. And
the pricing strategy itself precludes a consumer-pull,
advertising-driven launch. There just aren't enough margin points available.*

*This is why a brand like Suave, hugely dominant in
U.S. hair-care volume, can't even make it in Canada,
despite several attempts. Colgate's Palmolive hair-care
brand is in a similar position, except its home countries
are in the Spanish-speaking world. Henkel's Schauma is
another low-priced brand that can't travel, this time from
Germany.*

ment. P&G is the world leader here, mostly with its Head
& Shoulders brand. Antidandruff, historically, has been a

core category for global expansion. Unfortunately for P&G, it solves a problem that tends to go away as economies develop; the problem disappears as consumers increase their shampooing frequency.

The very biggest companies can focus on multiple categories. Here the key is to make sure those categories are strategically aligned. P&G's core fabric-care business has significant technical, manufacturing, and sourcing synergies with its hair-care business, helping both categories become world beaters. Technical strengths are particularly important, whether related to product formulation, engineering, or processing. Technology-based value-added is much more difficult to preempt than a price positioning or even a concept-only advantage.

Brand Selection

The major consumer product companies have accumulated many brands in each category they compete in, sometimes a dozen or more. Whether as a carryover from the days of frequent new-brand launches, excessive "Country Cowboy" autonomy, or via multiple acquisitions, their global portfolios often look like a dog's breakfast. Those portfolios make more sense upon closer examination, once you rule out the tiny brands and the brands that have slightly different names in different countries for trademark reasons—for example, Axe/Lynx deodorant from Unilever or Tide/Ariel detergent from P&G. Taking these into account, there are usually just three or four core brands, even in a company's top category.

Selling Out

As part of their strategy of simplification for global marketing, many major consumer product companies have been selling off small brands, even in core categories. Usually they sell to small manufacturers that quickly fail in their efforts to resuscitate them. After a failed attempt to expand the Lilt home-permanent brand into shampoo and conditioner, P&G sold the venerable brand to Dep (now owned by Henkel). Dep is still gamely trying to do something with Lilt but has little to show for its efforts. Gillette sold White Rain shampoo to a private-label company that is similarly floundering with it.

Sometimes, however, selling a brand comes back to haunt the seller. P&G sold off White Cloud toilet paper, a decent-sized business that had fairly high consumer awareness, although no real market differentiation. It has now become the controlled brand of toilet paper at Wal-Mart and is a significant competitor to P&G's market-leading Charmin brand. P&G sold Clearasil, the leading brand in the acne segment, to its biggest retail customer in the United Kingdom, Boots. Boots quickly hired a former P&G executive to restart growth on the brand in all its markets, including the United States. Meanwhile, the U.S. acne segment was in the process of merging with the regular facial-care category. The result is that P&G now has a major customer *attacking its quasi-acne Noxema*

(continued)

brand with a former P&G brand. It will be interesting to see if P&G's Olay brand follows L'Oreal, Aveeno, and other adult facial brands into acne. If it does, this will be the first time a major consumer product company has created a pincer movement against itself.

Here are suggestions for selecting a brand from within an identified core category to launch into a new market:

- Start at the top of the food chain, that is, at the high end of the market. L'Oreal's Garnier Division was launched in the United States with three high-priced, technology-intensive brands of hair color. Although none of these brands has been a huge hit, collectively they have established decent category credentials. Garnier is now leveraging this high-end credibility to launch a mainstream brand into the huge shampoo and conditioner market, something that would have been nearly impossible without its toehold in the hair-color category.
- Start with a brand that has been created relatively recently. Newer brands have several advantages when geographic expansion is the objective. Older brands tend to be conceptually flabby. They may have been the object of too many line extensions and have lost their salient points of differentiation. Instead, they rely on their established position, economies of scale, and inertia to retain their market share. Even if they've been managed with rigor, the original consumer insight and need that led to their early

success may have become less relevant. Cavity-fighting oral-care brands such as Crest face this dilemma. Fluoridation, floss, and more frequent brushing have watered down the impact of its "Look, Ma, no cavities" positioning. In addition, older brands have often been preempted by local marketers' imitators many years before.

- Go with the best brand name. Nothing is more important in marketing consumer products than the brand name. Nothing. This is true when your market is just one country. It's even truer when your market is global. It's extremely difficult to come up with a great brand name for use in just one country or language, never mind one that can span multiple countries or languages. The faux pas foisted on the world by Anglo-centric marketers are famous. The Chevy Nova, translated as "no go" in Latin

English as Artifact

An interesting challenge of globalization results from the proliferation of English words used out of context in much of Asia. Often, this meaningless English is used as a mere design element and is not intended to convey any specific verbal message. In Japan, you see and hear random English words in much of the advertising. A model for a wholesome product that is currently being advertised in Japan wears a shirt with the word hardcore *emblazoned across her chest. It's just there to look good, like a fleur-de-lis.*

America, is a classic of the genre. If you're fortunate to have a globally meaningful brand name at your disposal, that factor needs to weigh heavily in your expansion decision.

• Go with the brand name that has the best chance of creating global trademark unity. It is not absolutely essential to have the same brand name in every country. In fact, there are still a few brands in the United States that use different trademarks in different parts of the country. Edy's/Dreyer's ice cream and Hellmann's/Best Foods mayonnaise are examples. But you should try very hard to get trademark unity if at all possible, even if you have to buy out foreign trademark owners. Germany's Beiersdorf spent half a century rebuying its Nivea trademark in countries where it had been lost due to war repara-

Trademark Buying

Be careful about buying trademark rights speculatively. In other words, make sure the brand is successful in its lead market before committing large sums for the trademark in an expansion market. P&G recently paid an incredible eight-digit sum for the Physique hair-care trademark for use in Europe. By the time the deal was signed, Physique was already well on its way to failing, at great financial cost, in the United States.

tions. Nivea's long string of strong growth suggests that this was a good strategy.

- Go with the brand that best matches your company's size and reach. If you're marketing for a global consumer product company, you have the flexibility to enter either a huge category segment or a smaller one. You can afford the larger war. If, on the other hand, you're marketing for a smaller player, you almost certainly need to start with a small segment. Make sure you don't doom your plans from the start by spreading yourself too thin.

Selecting Countries for Expansion

The general list of criteria for selecting new countries to enter is a long one. It includes political stability, tax rates, labor practices, monetary policy, and so on. The following criteria are the key marketing-driven ones you need to keep in mind when picking your next market.

Language

Marketing, and particularly advertising, are first and foremost language-driven disciplines. It's all about nuances. Developing a bone-deep consumer understanding in any language, even your mother tongue, is very difficult. It's almost impossible to do so in a second language. Your ear for how a brand name or other brand communication sounds in a foreign language will almost always be just a bit off. Different languages reflect not just different ways of communicating but also different ways of thinking about and seeing the world.

Of course, you can deal with multiple languages by employing native speakers from each language you want to market in. But this is costly, both directly and indirectly. Multiple-language marketing is slow and error prone. It has an inevitable leveling effect, rounding off the edges of marketing communications. To the extent your business is marketing driven, you should push hard to use linguistic unity as a key criterion for geographical selection.

Maximum linguistic unity also helps with other aspects of your business besides marketing. It helps your company recruit and train people. It helps you work with retailer and supplier partners. It helps management create and commu-

English at Headquarters

For better and worse, English is the language of wider communication in the global business world. It's the official language of Swiss-based Nestlé, even though natives of that country speak German, French, and Italian. Most major German and Nordic companies, including Beiersdorf, Henkel, and Nokia, use English as their official language as well. Japanese companies communicate with their mainland Asian subsidiaries in English. Even the French are succumbing to the indispensability of English as the language of business.

nicate a company vision. When it comes to languages, fewer is certainly better.

For a U.S.-based consumer product company that is just starting to go global, the opening geographic moves are pretty obvious: Latangloland. That's my shorthand for the region comprising Latin America and the Anglophone countries. It's way too late to join the end-of-communism land grabs in Eastern Europe and East Asia. The maturity and competitiveness of mainland Europe make that market a poor choice. But Canada is a no-brainer, especially under NAFTA and following Wal-Mart's entry there. If you hire good English-speaking Canadians, they should be able to help you hire good French speakers and marketers for the seven million Quebecois. The first non-English language your organization needs to master is Spanish. Start with the thirty million U.S. Hispanics, a country within a country, complete with their own media channels and marketing infrastructure. The people and capabilities you develop here can serve as a bridge to your next geography. If you haven't started marketing to U.S. Hispanics yet, you're not ready for the rest of Latin America. When you're ready, Mexico (especially following NAFTA's signing, Wal-Mart's entry, and President Fox's election) needs to be your next move.

After Mexico, the choices get far less clear. Your key options are to work your way through the rest of Latin America or through the rest of the English-speaking world. Neither option is easy. In much of Latin America, poverty and instability are major obstacles. In the United Kingdom and Ireland, the trade clout, prevalence of private label, and presence of almost every single global player can make that market a financial black hole. On balance, though, the United Kingdom should probably get the nod, especially given Wal-Mart's large-scale entry, via its acquisition of ASDA.

Size and Growth

As important as language considerations are in selecting geographies to compete in, language is far from the only factor that should influence your decisions. Attractive geographical markets include those that are large enough to sustain your brands and those that are growing in the right areas. Population is important but not as important as having a population affluent enough to afford your class of products. Gross domestic product (GDP) does a decent job of indicating levels of affluence.

Even better than straight GDP is GDP that is adjusted for purchasing power. This factors in both income and relative costs. Looking at income distribution can also be help-

Visualize Economic Size

Through The Economist, *you can get maps that use GDP rather than square miles to portray the size of each country. They are quite enlightening to look at. Japan is portrayed as being ten times bigger than India, for example.*

ful. It's better to enter a market with many middle-class consumers than one with the same GDP but most of the income going to super-rich oligarchs. Economists have devised a fairly precise measure of relative income distribution, called the Gini coefficient, to help to measure this.

Although size certainly matters, so does growth. The economies of continental Europe and Japan may be huge, but they are also mature. Japan, in fact, has been suffering through more than ten years of sales contraction in most business sectors, including consumer products.

Category-Specific Factors

The relative size and growth of specific product categories varies dramatically by geography, irrespective of such factors as GDP and per-capita income. Sometimes the varying degrees of category development, even within a country, are immense—with no obvious explanation. Bostonians consume an extraordinary amount of chocolate, for example. Comfort food to stave off Red Sox blues? Puritan-heritage guilt? Who knows?

In many cases, however, you can find an explanation for variations in category development. The main cause may be cultural factors, such as religion. For example, nobody is going to make a lot of money marketing beef to India's Hindu population. Consumption of many other foods is influenced by culture. Another cause of variation is the climate. Body lotions don't sell well in humid Britain or Japan. Sometimes differences in category development are based on subtle differences such as hardness of water and water pressure. Such mundane issues as plumbing partially explain the differences in shower or bathing habits from country to country. These habits, in turn, influence things like preferences for bar soaps over body washes.

In light of these differences, you are looking for countries and regions where your chosen category and brand have the potential to be large and growing. Be extra careful about the data you gather on this. In particular, make sure the research service you use classifies products similarly to the way you do it in your home country. As is often the case, your best feel for category size and growth in many countries can come from a couple of well-planned days doing store checks with a local guide or colleague.

Channel-Specific Factors

It's difficult to master marketing to more than one broad channel. If you're a prestige marketer, you need to look for prestige channels you can use in new geographies. In many countries, such channels are either nonexistent or underdeveloped. In Canada, for example, the department store channel is so weak that Lancôme has been forced to sell its fifty-dollar potions through drugstores, right down the aisle from cheap and cheerful mass-market brands. When upper-end mass-market brands enter Germany and other European markets, they are forced to choose between upper mass and lower mass, a distinction that doesn't exist in the United States. These unique choices make it imperative that you clearly understand where your brand fits in the overall marketing universe.

Acquisitions

In the merger-and-acquisition heyday of the sixties and seventies, mindless diversification resulted in mass confusion. Consumer product companies found themselves way too deep in far more categories, businesses, and countries than they could reasonably manage. Coca-Cola, for example, even stepped briefly into the movie studio business. Today there is still occasionally a random acquisition such as P&G's purchase of a dog food company a couple of years ago (even as the company was exiting human food). However, most consumer product companies are now wisely focusing on being strong on a global scale in just a few categories. I call this packing the snowball tighter.

Acquisitions helped Colgate set the stage on which it finally regained leadership in the U.S. toothpaste market from P&G's Crest. Colgate did this by making numerous acquisitions of overseas toothpaste brands, including the leading brand in South America. Despite P&G's prior purchase of Blendax, a major European oral-care competitor, the company couldn't muster the commitment, critical mass, or technical innovation to stave off the resurgence of Colgate in its flagship and namesake category.

L'Oreal's purchase of U.S.-based Maybelline (from a company that should never have owned it in the first place,

Schering Plough) was an excellent strategic fit. The acquisition gave L'Oreal corporate leadership in its core category—cosmetics—in the world's most important established market. It also gave L'Oreal a calling card to penetrate China, the world's most important developing market. L'Oreal, the quintessentially French company, is now run by a Brit who sells French cachet to the United States and American cachet to the Chinese. This is strategic marketing at its best.

Managing Global Brands

A relatively small handful of brands has made the full transition from national to global. Coke, Sony, McDonald's, Nike, and Disney make this short list. So do Colgate, Pantene, Nivea, Johnson's Baby, and Gillette. Yet achieving global status yields significant competitive advantage only if the transition is managed with discipline and imagination. Here are some suggestions for doing so:

- Make sure global strategic leadership for the brand is identified clearly, staffed well, and empowered. Although listening is a key skill in global marketing, business is not a democracy. The global category wars are won only with decisive and powerful generals at the helm.
- Embrace the idea of lead markets. Not all geographies are of equal strategic importance. Some are important because of their sheer profit potential. Others punch

above their weight because they logically serve as the lead market for a whole cluster of other countries. Still others are important because they can serve as affordable but representative test markets for new initiatives.

- Don't waste global meeting time with information sharing. Information such as market data, advertising creative, financial results, and new-product launches should be readily and instantaneously available online. The only constraint on information sharing should be time. When global teams do get together—either in person, via videoconferencing, or even through old-fashioned teleconferencing—all players should already be familiar with the basic data. Meeting time should be spent creatively on issues, opportunities, plans, and team building.

- Pay special attention to the chronology of market entry. If a brand is quite new in a market, its needs are very different from those of a brand in a market where it has been long established. In the newer market, for example, the marketing imperative could still be to gain trial. In a more established market where a product's trial level is already high, the focus may be on increased product loyalty or cross-product purchasing.

- The brands with the largest market share may not have the best marketing model to follow. There are myriad reasons why a given brand will have a greater share in one country than in others. Often, the reasons have nothing to do with marketing. A brand may be getting the

The Price of Fun

I have worked at several companies where the U.K. marketers believed they were far superior to their U.S. counterparts. In some cases, this was certainly true. But in general, the United Kingdom's relative marketplace success had more to do with the fact that marketers simply did not introduce the brands that failed in their U.S. "test market." All the money their American colleagues spent on failed new products went into shoring up core U.K. brands.

Of course, success breeds autonomy, even in advertising creative. And since the United Kingdom is just a bit too small to easily justify quantitative copy testing, most creative decisions are made there on judgment alone or with a thin scrim of focus group research. My hypothesis is that this is why Britain leads the world in hilarious, award-winning, "I wonder what brand that ad was for?" creative. It very well may be commercially useless. But since nearly every U.K. brand uses the same approach, there's no real competitive disadvantage in this. And, oh, what fun!

benefits of a low-cost infrastructure, including manufacturing and sales, that allow it to invest more in advertising, for example.

CMO Checkpoints

1. Globalization is an on-the-ground reality in almost every consumer product category. Embrace it.
2. Globalization requires that you simplify your category portfolio, your number of marketing channels, or both.
3. Whatever else you do, focus on being the global champ in at least one category of significance.
4. Remember that technology advantages travel to new geographies much better than price or even conceptual ones. If you have superior technology in an area, leverage it broadly and quickly, before it gets preempted.
5. When picking new geographies to expand into, keep the number of languages as small as possible. Marketing and advertising are language-driven disciplines.
6. Marketing is also a name game. Don't settle for using a second-rate name as your global moniker, even if you have to buy a first-rate trademark.
7. Once a brand becomes global, the people management side of the business becomes even more critical to success. Listen to each market, but don't forget the importance of central leadership on strategic issues.

Lesson ***10***

The Future of Marketing

There has never been a better time to be in consumer product marketing—and we're just getting started. Innovative breakthroughs in product development, consumer insight creation, and retailer micromarketing promise to make the next several decades not only incredibly productive, but absorbingly interesting.

Product Innovation

The consumer product industry is becoming more and more driven by true product innovation. Great progress is being made. Much of this innovation shows up in the form of higher quality or lower prices. And much of it takes the form of better benefit delivery. Dish-washing liquids wipe cleaner than ever before. Lipsticks look better and stay on longer. Diapers leak less. And even fat-free foods taste better than ever. The mousetraps are indeed getting better.

In the future, consumer product companies' focus on product innovation will get sharper and sharper as they become more global minded and more concentrated on fewer product categories. The absolute R&D dollars per category per company will increase. Product innovation will flourish. Innovation is the fundamental reason for the existence of consumer product companies. Power retailers can't do it. Private-label manufacturers can't do it. It's our domain.

The logic of innovation is compelling. True product innovation dramatically reduces marketing costs; low-cost publicity can substitute for much of the extraordinarily expensive launch media. True product innovation is the easiest thing to export into global markets; functionality is a universal language. And true product innovation is becoming easier for strategically committed companies; the tools and educational capital are more abundant than ever.

Much of the coming innovation will continue to be incremental. Childproof packaging that adults can open. Mouthwash that stops odor for a week. But there will also be the occasional shot at the moon—a product that cures obesity, eliminates insomnia, improves vision, or permanently reduces pain or extends life expectancy. It's going to be exciting. Marketers, long accustomed to eking out share gains without the benefit of major product innovation, will need to raise not only their own sights but those of everyone in their organization.

Epoch-making innovation that delivers profound consumer satisfaction requires tightly focused resources, but it also demands new mind-sets, new incentive systems, new management structures, and a new kind of leadership. In other words, it requires purposeful innovation in the area of organizational design.

Product Innovation Through Technical Brand Management

Many companies are creating a new role—the technical brand manager. People in this position have the knowledge and skill sets to effectively link core, brand-relevant consumer needs with applicable technical leads. They have the knowledge to discuss technical issues deeply. And they have the ability to translate expressed consumer needs into actionable technical direction. All too often, nontechnical marketers are so pushed and pulled by the daily pressure of commercial imperatives that they develop only a superficial knowledge of technology development. On the other hand, most project leaders who come out of R&D or engineering can't decipher the nonlinear, subtle language consumers use to describe their core, underlying needs. What's more, many of these technical people simply don't like or even respect the commercial side of the business.

The creation of a successful technical brand management system will take innovation in education, recruiting, training, and career development. Most importantly, it will take incentives to force high-potential candidates to make temporarily lateral moves into areas where they have little current expertise. Long term, it will take the example of rewarding people on this track with promotions to top management. The globalization imperative of the past twenty years has produced many CEOs with multicultural experience. Today's and tomorrow's product innovation imperative can and must similarly produce CEOs with deep multifunctional expertise. In the interim, we should start getting used to the idea of technical brand directors and even technical brand VPs.

Product Innovation Through Outsourcing

The best consumer product companies are already operating on a virtual basis in many areas. Any function that is not considered both mission-critical and a source of competitive advantage is being scrutinized for outsourcing. R&D has long been outsourced by small sales- and marketing-driven companies. In fact, one of the key reasons big companies buy these smaller companies is so that the big companies can apply their technology to the smaller company's brands. Increasingly, however, even the largest and most technology-driven of consumer product companies are effectively outsourcing a significant amount of R&D. The heads of R&D are becoming conductors of an entire symphony of technical resources. P&G acquired the Spinbrush business for its technology. P&G simply applied its distribution clout and Crest brand name to make Crest

Spinbrush a huge hit. (This was also a great example of innovation requiring very little media. Publicity and in-store demonstrations did the trick.)

Many companies are now outsourcing some of their technology development to universities. Shiseido even gave Harvard University an outright $10 million research grant to get on the inside. The University of Michigan is part of many industry-sponsored hair-care studies. The University of Pennsylvania is a major player in skin-care research.

Industry players are increasingly leveraging their trade associations to conduct jointly sponsored research through outside suppliers. This is especially common in cases where health or safety is a factor. Collaboration not only reduces costs, it also increases the perceived objectivity and thus credibility of the findings. The Cosmetics, Toiletries and Fragrance Association's continuing work on ingredient safety is a good example.

Product Innovation Through Joint Ventures

So far, most attempts at joint technology development between consumer product companies have failed. Their failure stems from the fact that most of the work is applied research rather than basic research. Thus, partners end up fighting for control of the applications. No examples of joint ventures driven by consumer product technology are comparable to Dow Corning. For decades, the Dow Chemical Company and Corning (the glass company) have shared the benefits of this highly innovative joint venture. In consumer products, cross-licensing of patents is about as close as it gets. An example is patent sharing of individual hair dyes between Henkel and L'Oreal. Less publicly, even joint research projects between divisions of huge consumer product companies fail at least as often as they succeed.

In the future, consumer product companies will get better at picking projects and partners for technology-driven joint ventures. We should be looking for partners in adjacent categories that are not on the verge of entering our own categories. We should look at joint development of technologies that have fewer potential conflicts than specific product technologies. S. C. Johnson, for example, has made it clear that it will stay out of the personal-care market to focus on household products. Given the strength and

The Technology Marketplace

The innovation imperative is so important that companies are going to extreme lengths to economically justify and support research. There are now sales companies established for the sole purpose of helping clients sell or license their patents and other proprietary knowledge or intellectual property on the open market. The website for one such company, featuring listings from Johnson & Johnson, General Mills, Kao, P&G and many others, is www .yet2.com. P&G, which has set up an entire sales organization for this purpose, claims its tech hawking now brings in as much profit as a billion-dollar brand would generate.

size of its aerosol business—for brands such as Raid and Glade—S. C. Johnson would be an ideal joint venture partner for a company focused on, say, hair spray.

Consumer Insights

Marketing research must and will discover ways to quantitatively link individual consumer purchase and usage behavior with media consumption and expressed attitudes. The current tools get at isolated bits and pieces of this, but none of them bring it all together. The lack of an integrated information system makes it hard for researchers to unearth meaningful consumer insights in the first place. When researchers do generate an insight, the lack of an integrated information system makes proving the validity of the insight painfully slow and provisional.

Some newly evolving tools may help. Here are some examples:

- Media tracking is starting to go beyond in-home measurement. Consumer panelists in one experiment wear what is essentially an electronic tattoo. This device tracks their entire consumption of electronic media, regardless of whether it takes place at home, in the car, or at a bar.
- The Web has firmly established itself as a cost-effective research tool. Most concept testing is already done online. With broadband connections and low-cost, PC-based videoconferencing, reliable qualitative research will become possible. (When consumers are talking about

how they feel, you simply must see them.) The Internet will also enable such product-specific research as fragrance research in the relatively near future. Low-cost digital fragrance emitters are already being patented.

- Many consumer marketers, most impressively Coty, are now selling some of their products through their websites. Even on a small scale, this direct transactional relationship can be invaluable. It can, for example, help with refining advertising messages. As Web users become more and more representative of the population at large, this—and other uses of the Internet for research—will just get better.

- A large proportion of consumer product companies' online spending now goes to old-fashioned co-op trade ads. Drugstore.com and other online retailers still charge manufacturers fixed rates for online ads, much the way CVS and Walgreens do for their newspaper-delivered advertising fliers. This is a major lost opportunity for retailers and manufacturers alike. In the future, online retailers can and will find a way to charge marketers based on sales of their products, not ad space. That pricing structure will turn this small but growing class of trade into a significant new source of consumer insights.

- The large holes in the scanner data universe will gradually get plugged. B.J.'s, the smallest wholesale club, now provides scanner data. Costco and Sam's Club may do the same. And UPCs—just country codes today—may finally start living up to their "universal" name. In addition, it is possible that scanner data will finally be able to tell manufacturers something as simple as their level of distribution. Right now, all the data can tell manufacturers is how many stores are scanning products, not how many have the products on their shelves. Remote radio wave scanning of entire store inventories may be coming. An added benefit will be accurate reporting of in-store displays.

- It's possible that the Web will enable the creation of the long-sought-after one-to-one relationship between a brand and its core users. This will involve fully personalized bundles of brand values that go well beyond the physical product. We know consumers already use brands as a means of defining and expressing themselves. They are part of consumers' psychological wardrobe. Beauty-care retailer Reflect.com provides a level of customization—including a choice of fragrances and graphic designs, plus the consumer's very own name on the package—not possible in a bricks-and-mortar model. Reflect.com also sends flowers—lots of them. While it doesn't look like the economics are going to work out for Reflect.com or similar ventures such as Levi's attempt to sell totally tailored jeans, the consumer insights gained probably can be applied to a more practical channel.

Retailer Micromarketing

In the future, it will be easier than ever to get innovative, well-marketed brands in the hands of very tightly defined consumer groups. Retailers are getting incredibly good at

Consumption-Linked Media

Imagine a world in which your refrigerator automatically reorders groceries, making product on demand a reality. Imagine, too, that the refrigerator is digitally connected to your TV, which tracks exactly what programming you consume. If all works out, the only ads you would see would be ads for either the products you already are buying or ones that your purchase patterns suggests you'd be highly likely to buy. And the marketer of these products will only have to spend ad money on the programs you view.

Many consumers would undoubtedly consider such advances an invasion of privacy and would opt out. But for others, the benefits would be significant. Imagine watching the evening news and seeing ads for products you are interested in rather than the parade of irrelevant (to you) ads you now have to sit through. Imagine the money you'd save if you didn't have to pay, indirectly, for the wasted advertising dollars that are currently invested by marketers. And imagine how much you'd save on your cable bill if you got charged for only the programs you watched, especially if you opted to allow ads to run on them.

micromarketing. The best of them are adjusting their product assortment on a store-by-store basis. The customization is based on far more than the traditional traits of store size and trading-area affluence. Retailers now use traits like age, ethnicity, lifestyle, and a whole host of other variables. Just as important, the level of individual store compliance with a predetermined segmentation plan is far higher than just a few years ago. In other words, the shelves look the way they are intended to look far more often than in even the recent past.

The net result of retailers' improved ability to micromarket at the store level is that consumer product marketers can tailor their offerings as never before. The velocity threshold of x pieces per store per week is more important than ever. What's changed is that it is now OK to achieve threshold velocity in just a portion of total stores. If you've got a product that only (or primarily) appeals to African-Americans, for example, you no longer need to worry about its chainwide average velocity. You just need to be concerned about its velocity in the specific stores within the chain that carry it.

The challenge is to effectively generate consumer demand for a product that is in only partial distribution. Sometimes, such as in the African-American example just used, existing consumer promotion and media vehicles—such as *Essence* magazine and the BET network—are already available. In other cases, such as nasal spray distributed only in stores with rapid turnover of anti-allergy products, you need to improvise. There isn't an all-allergy cable channel (yet). Another possibility is piggybacking on retailers' store-by-store communications for their frequent-

Home-Delivery Micromarketing

Improved store-by-store micromarketing and shelf-set compliance are helping traditional self-service bricks-and-mortar stores provide better customization. Similarly, big improvements are being made by their online, home-delivery counterparts. Home delivery of consumer products is nothing new. The Sears catalog pioneered this concept 150 years ago. What is new are the radical improvements in the ordering and receiving processes.

There have been a number of high-profile failures of Internet-driven home delivery, but Peapod (now owned by power retailer Ahold) and other innovative grocers are leveraging technology to make home delivery viable for a narrow group of upscale, time-starved consumers. Software not only makes it easy to shop for groceries online but makes reordering intuitive and fast. Online grocers guarantee delivery within a narrow band of time. They even make it easy to use coupons. Their pick-pack-ship operations are becoming fully automated, allowing the efficient use of customized totes for each household. Leading-edge online grocers are taking the next logical step of installing coolers at customers' homes, eliminating the need for consumers to be home to receive goods. Give it a try yourself.

As a side note, it's interesting that syndicated—that is multiple-vendor—home delivery of groceries is in many ways a return to the past. Remember the milkman? Tech-

nology has made this delivery model viable again. It won't replace the dominant self-service, bricks-and-mortar model for more than a couple of percentage points of consumer product sales. But for most consumer products, it is far more appropriate than the much-hyped direct-marketing models that ultimately rely on outsiders—either the U.S. Postal Service or vendor-by-vendor shippers such as UPS—to deliver the products. The U.S. Postal Service is simply not a cost-effective channel partner for most consumer products. I am constantly reminding my marketing teams that the CPM (cost per thousand) for anything that ends up in the mail is $300 just for the stamps.

shopper programs. Also, you need to make sure the in-store communication, especially the package, sells the targeted benefits very clearly.

Consumer product marketing is still in its infancy, just a couple of generations old in its modern sense. The future will bring an explosion of product innovation, actionable consumer insights, and rapid improvements in customized delivery. The consumer will win—a little more profoundly every year. Let's go!

CMO Checkpoints

1. Product innovation will increase significantly in the near future, reducing marketing costs as well as revving up

revenues. Marketers must take the lead by raising the sights of their entire organization. Some of us will need to get more tech-savvy, while our R&D counterparts will need to get more commercial.

2. The Internet has the potential to transform consumer marketers' ability to discover and experiment with new consumer insights. Don't forget to leverage the insight potential of already-established transactional websites. And get ready to do online qualitative research once the technology matures a bit further.

3. Although the self-service, bricks-and-mortar approach to retailing will continue to dominate consumer products, syndicated home delivery will likely grow as a channel for the time-starved, upscale consumer segment. Be alert to the consumer insights that can come from this new distribution mechanism.

4. Retail stores are getting better at micromarketing, particularly in terms of store-by-store shelf setting and in-store compliance. Consider leveraging micromarketing to more tightly target smaller consumer segments, especially those with well-defined micromedia vehicles.

Index

Index

Index

Index

Michaels, Al, 110
Micromarketing
  home-delivery, 234–35
  retailers, 231–35
Mitchell, Paul, hair care, 123
M&M, 122
Modular review, 131
MRI, 31, 92
Mrs. Dash, 58
Murdoch, Rupert, 6

NAFTA, 213
NBC, 115
Nestlé, 22, 163, 212
Network feeds, 97
Neutral pricing, 182
Neutrogena, 160
New brands, 161–63
Newman, Paul, salad dressing, 123
New products, 153–74, 219
  creating successful, 163–68
  launch of, 170–73
  profit margins and, 177–78
  types of, 153–163
News America, 147
News Corporation, 6
Newsworthiness, 108–9
Nielsen, 17, 31, 44, 48, 50, 58
Nike, 65, 123, 218
Nivea, 211, 218
Noxell, 19

Off-shelf displays, 160
Olay, 4, 63, 182
Old Spice, 11, 183
On-camera talent, 81
One-on-ones, 34
One-to-one relationship, 231
Online focus groups, 33
Online grocers, 234
Oreos, 162
Outsourcing, 226–27

Packaging, 11–12, 19
  impact on product performance, 43
  improvements in, 157
Packaging-based publicity, 121–22

Panel-based scanner data, 49–51
Pantene, 12, 185, 204–5
Papa John, 75
Parkay, 123
Pass-along rates, 103
Passion, 21–26
Patents, cross-licensing of, 227–28
Payment deductions, 142
Payment terms, 140–141
Pepsi, 5, 15, 43, 59, 62, 65, 123, 182
Pert, 12
Physique hair care, 163
Piggybacking, 160
Pillsbury, 14, 77
Planograms, 131
Point-of-sale (POS) data, 48
Positioning complex brands, 63–64
Positioning statement, 64
Pragmatic method, 87, 91–92
Preferred page positioning, 104
Premium pricing, 183
President's Choice, 159
Press kit, 116
Price increases, 187–0
  via size reductions, 189–90
Price per placement, 102–3
Pricing, 134
  on acquired and new brands, 185
  changing, 186
  components of, 186–87
  line, 191
  low-road, 183–85
  neutral, 182
  premium, 183
  service-based, 141
  strategies for, 181–90
Procter & Gamble, 4, 5, 12, 13, 14–15, 19,
  20, 21, 55, 146, 147, 151–52, 155,
  163, 172, 183, 184, 185, 200, 201,
  202, 203, 204–6, 207, 210, 217,
  226–27, 228
Product-based publicity, 121–22
Product innovation, 223–29
  through joint ventures, 227–28
  through outsourcing, 226–27
  through technical brand management,
    225–26

241

Index

About the Author

Bradford C. Kirk is the chief marketing officer of the Andrew Jergens Company, the Cincinnati-based consumer product subsidiary of Japan's Kao Corporation. Previously, Mr. Kirk was the chief marketing officer of the Consumer Products Division of Unilever's Helene Curtis, the Home Entertainment Division of News Corporation's Twentieth Century Fox, and the Consumer Products Division of the Alberto-Culver Company. During a twenty-two-year career in consumer product marketing, he has championed such brands as Jergens, Curél, Bioré, St. Ives Swiss Formula, John Frieda Sheer Blonde, Salon Selectives, Finesse, Suave, Alberto VO5, FDS, Ban, and Degree health- and beauty-care products; Meow Mix, Whisker Lickin's, Mrs. Dash, Molly McButter, and Static Guard food/household products; and *Independence Day*, *X-Files*, *Shirley Temple*, and *Star Wars* home videos.

Mr. Kirk has an MBA degree from Northwestern University's Kellogg Graduate School of Management. He can be contacted at bradfordkirk@hotmail.com.